from INSPIRATION
to LEGISLATION

How an Idea Becomes a Bill

REAL POLITICS IN AMERICA

Series Editor: Paul S. Herrnson, *University of Maryland*

The books in this series bridge the gap between academic scholarship and the popular demand for knowledge about politics. They illustrate empirically supported generalization from original research and the academic literature using examples taken from the legislative process, executive branch decision making, court rulings, lobbying efforts, election campaigns, political movements, and other areas of American politics. The goal of the series is to convey the best contemporary political science research has to offer in ways that will engage individuals who want to know about real politics in America.

from INSPIRATION *to* LEGISLATION

How an Idea Becomes a Bill

Amy E. Black

PEARSON

Prentice
Hall

Upper Saddle River, New Jersey 07458

Library of Congress Cataloging-in-Publication Data

Black, Amy E.
    From inspiration to legislation : how an idea becomes a bill / Amy E. Black.
      p. cm. — (Real politics in America)
    Includes index.
    ISBN-13: 978-0-13-110754-0 (alk. paper)
    ISBN-10: 0-13-110754-2 (alk. paper)
    1. Legislation—United States. 2. Bill drafting—United States. I. Title. II. Series.
    KF4945.B53 2006
    328.73'0772—dc22

                                                                    2006010248

Editorial Director: Charlyce Jones Owen
Acquisitions Editor: Dickson Musslewhite
Editorial Assistant: Jennifer Murphy
Marketing Manager: Emily Cleary
Marketing Assistant: Jennifer Lang
Director of Production and
    Manufacturing: Barbara Kittle
Managing Editor: Lisa Iarkowski
Production Liaison: Joe Scordato
Production Assistant: Marlene Gassler
Prepress and Manufacturing Manager:
    Nick Sklitsis

Prepress and Manufacturing Buyer:
    Mary Ann Gloriande
Cover Art Director: Jayne Conte
Cover Design: Kiwi Design
Composition/Full Service Project
    Management: GGS Production
    Services/Karpagam Jagadeesan
Printer/Binder: RR Donnelley & Sons, Inc.
Cover Printer: RR Donnelley & Sons, Inc.
Cover Photo: Courtesy of Office of
    Congresswoman Melissa A. Hart
    (PA-04)

This book was set in 10/12 Palatino.
Real Politics in America
Series Editor: Paul S. Herrnson

Credits and acknowledgments borrowed from other sources and reproduced, with permission, in this textbook appear on appropriate page within text.

Pearson Education LTD.
Pearson Education Singapore, Pte. Ltd
Pearson Education, Canada, Ltd
Pearson Education—Japan

Pearson Education Australia PTY, Limited
Pearson Education North Asia Ltd
Pearson Educacion de Mexico, S.A. de C.V.
Pearson Education Malaysia, Pte. Ltd

10 9 8 7 6 5 4 3 2 1
ISBN 0-13-110754-2

To John J. Pitney Jr.
Adviser, Mentor, Role Model, and Friend

Contents

CHAPTER 8

FINDING A WAY TO THE FLOOR: A BILL
BECOMES TWO LAWS   105

APPENDIX A

★ PREFACE

Breaking away from the crowds at an annual gathering of thousands of political scientists, my undergraduate adviser and I strolled down the streets of San Francisco looking for a coffee shop. After ordering our drinks, we settled down for our annual chat during the meetings of the American Political Science Association (APSA), a conversation I anticipate each year when Jack Pitney and I can talk about the past year of academic life.

This was a particularly momentous occasion for me, however, as I was updating my undergraduate adviser about my time working on Capitol Hill. The previous year, Jack had encouraged me to apply for an APSA Congressional Fellowship, a program designed to give academic political scientists much-needed practical experience in American politics. Supported by the program, fellows find work in congressional offices and spend almost a year working as legislative staff.

As we discussed my year in Washington working for Representative Melissa Hart, Jack asked me to summarize in a sentence the most important lesson I learned. I answered, "I understood the basic mechanics of how a bill becomes a law, but my time in D.C. helped me see how an idea becomes a bill." To this, my adviser replied, "That's not just a great lesson form your time on the Hill, that's a great idea for a book." Within minutes, we were on our way back to the hotel, deep in an animated discussion of a concept that would become this book.

American government textbooks almost always include a diagram that offers some variation on the theme of how a bill becomes a law. In a neat chart with boxes and arrows, such diagrams trace the path of a bill from its introduction through the official channels of the legislative process. Such a flowchart, however, skips to the middle of the story and fails to introduce many of the key actors who influence the process. By starting at the very beginning with the initial idea that inspires legislation and following it as legislators and their staff craft the concept into a bill, this book tells a more complete story of the beginning of the legislative process and the work of those individuals who translate ideas into bills.

Compared to so many complex and contentious bills before Congress, H.R. 2018, the Safe Havens Support Act, was a "small" bill addressing a simple but poignant issue: the problem of newborn babies left to die in trash dumpsters, portable toilets, or even snowdrifts. Newly elected Congresswoman Melissa Hart arrived in Washington determined that Congress needed to pass legislation to help states in their work to prevent infant abandonment. She knew that members would join in general agreement with the policy goal of such legislation; the true challenge would come in crafting a solution and funding mechanism that both conservatives and liberals would accept and support.

From Inspiration to Legislation follows the Safe Havens Support Act from the initial policy idea that inspired the bill through its crafting and eventual passage as part of two larger bills. Relying on participant observation and on documents collected while I worked for Representative Hart, this book examines the ground-level challenges of a new member developing a legislative agenda and offers readers an insider's view of the daily work of a congressional office, the political process, and the development of legislation.

This book would not be possible without the help of mentors who have encouraged me in my career and helped shape my understanding of politics. My undergraduate adviser, John J. Pitney Jr., is a constant and faithful source of encouragement and sage advice. I also appreciate the help of my graduate adviser, Charles Stewart III, who introduced me to the study of Congress and helped me chart my path in the study of American politics.

I owe a debt of gratitude to Representative Melissa Hart and her staff, who welcomed me as part the team and trusted me to develop legislation. It was a privilege to work for a member whom I respect and appreciate as a person and as a legislator. Hart's staff made me feel a part of the office family. In particular, I am indebted to Bill Ries, Christian Marchant, Bill Rys, Eleas Phillips, Corry Marshall, and Brendan Benner, all of whom assisted me in countless ways.

This book would not have been possible without the APSA Congressional Fellowship Program and its director, Jeff Biggs. The year in Washington was transformational, broadening my understanding of the policymaking process and opening doors for continued conversation and interaction with members of Congress and their staff.

My work also benefited from the suggestions of the series editor, Paul Herrnson, and the team at Prentice Hall. Additional thanks to Christopher Upham, Erin Hoekstra, Josh Magnusson, and Jennifer Aycock for their capable research assistance and good humor throughout the process and to Gayle Boss and Dan Treier for their careful editing. Jan Miller, department secretary extraordinaire, was a wonderful source of encouragement and assistance. Support from the Wheaton College Alumni Fund and the G. W. Aldeen Fund helped make this book possible.

Finally, I am grateful to my family. My parents and my sister provided constant encouragement and support as I pursued the fellowship in Washington and as I wrote this book. My husband Dan joined the cheering section toward the end of this project, adding new dimensions of joy to my life and creating new motivations to complete my work. I am truly blessed to have such devoted fans.

Amy E. Black
Wheaton, Illinois

from INSPIRATION *to* LEGISLATION

How an Idea Becomes a Bill

INTRODUCTION

So You Want to Pass a Bill?

What does Representative Barbara Lee, the Berkeley, California, Democrat who cast the only vote in Congress against military action in Afghanistan in the aftermath of September 11, have in common with Representative Tom DeLay, the former Republican leader, nicknamed the "Hammer," who was one of the war's strongest advocates? Both were among seventy four other Republicans and Democrats in the 107th Congress who cosponsored H.R. 2018, the Safe Havens Support Act. What type of issue could unite these two members from opposite ends of the political spectrum? Lee and DeLay, along with many members of the liberal Congressional Black Caucus and the conservative Republican Study Committee, joined in support of legislation that encouraged the creation of safe havens for abandoned infants.

Lee, DeLay, and the political camps they represent sit on opposite sides of the controversial abortion debate. Although the chasm between the two sides usually seems insurmountable, supporters and opponents of abortion come to agreement on at least two things: women in crisis need help, and newborn babies deserve protection. The Safe Havens Support Act garnered bipartisan support from members on both sides of the abortion debate because it met pro-choice and pro-life activists at these points of near consensus, seeking to help scared mothers unable or unwilling to care for their newborns and to provide protection and loving homes for their babies.

Although many complex and contentious bills are introduced each congressional session, members of Congress translate hundreds of other ideas into "small" bills that address a simple issue or seek to correct technicalities in the law. While the headlines focus attention on the partisan wrangling and high theatrics of floor debate, the news media rarely take notice of these little bills that pass in the House of Representatives almost every legislative day.

This book tells the story of one such small bill, tracing H.R. 2018 from the kernel of an idea through its eventual passage as part of a larger social services bill. By focusing on how one legislator's idea became a bill and how that bill became a law, this book shows how legislation develops, how a congressional office works day to day, and how a freshman member of Congress newly arrived in Washington with a legislative agenda views the political process.

Before tracing the path of H.R. 2018, however, this chapter introduces the key players and central policy concerns that led to the development of this legislation. After introducing Congresswoman Melissa Hart, the lead sponsor of the Safe Havens Support Act, it also considers the central policy concerns that led to the development of this bill and describes the structure and role of the congressional staff necessary to turn a congresswoman's idea into a successful bill.

BREAKING DOWN BARRIERS: MELISSA HART'S ROAD TO WASHINGTON

In many ways, Melissa Hart is an unlikely politician. The granddaughter of union-supporting, coal-mining Democrats, Hart was born and raised outside Pittsburgh, Pennsylvania, the youngest of three children born to Don and Albina Hart. Don Hart had a strong influence on his family, teaching his children to value God, family, and hard work. Contrary to family tradition, however, Don Hart broke ranks with the Democratic Party. His daughter followed his lead; demonstrating Republican leanings from an early age, she wrote an eighth-grade essay, "Why Ronald Reagan Is a Patriot."[1] Don Hart died of a heart attack at age 49, an event that shaped the family's life profoundly. Until then a stay-at-home mom, Albina Hart went to work as a secretary to support her family, and all the children helped as they could.

Hart worked her way through Washington and Jefferson College, majoring in business and German, and then through law school at the University of Pittsburgh. While at Washington and Jefferson, Hart found herself one of a very few outspoken Republicans on campus. An active member of the Young Republicans in a heavily Democratic region, she discovered many opportunities to work directly with and for Republican candidates and began developing the political acumen and skills that would serve her in the coming years.

ENTERING POLITICS

After law school, Hart joined the Pittsburgh law firm of Hergenroeder and Heights, concentrating most of her practice on real estate law. Too restless to settle into a career practicing law, Hart soon set her sights on public office, deciding to challenge Democratic state senator John Regoli. Explaining her motivation to run, Hart said, "Often, the very first thing people talk about when you ask them is their taxes. . . . I never thought of running for office until a point in my life when I realized the money being taken from us wasn't being spent in an effective way."[2] Without strong party support, Hart relied on a grassroots campaign, knocking on doors throughout the district. Against the odds, she won the race. At age 28, the new senator arrived in Harrisburg, the only Republican woman in the senate chamber.

Hart went on to win reelection twice and move her way up the Republican ranks. She earned a post as chair of the Senate Finance Committee, a perfect platform for a tax reformer. Rankled after she lost a party leadership position, Hart saw an opportunity to make her next political move. Representative Ron Klink, a Democratic congressman from suburban Pittsburgh, announced he would vacate his congressional seat at the end of the term and challenge Republican Rick Santorum for the U.S. Senate. Klink's district, the solidly Democratic fourth district of Pennsylvania that wraps around northern Pittsburgh and winds west to the Ohio border, included part of Hart's state senate district and much of the area she called home. Ready for a new challenge and undaunted by the Democratic voting history of the area, Hart announced her campaign and began the door knocking once again. This time, fueled by a million-dollar-plus budget and help from the National Republican Congressional Committee, Hart once again defied history, capturing 59 percent of the vote and earning her place as the first Republican woman in the history of Pennsylvania elected to Congress.

Although Hart's path into politics as a Republican in a Democratically dominated region challenged the political odds, her grassroots campaigning style and desire to seek higher office followed a more conventional path for ambitious elected officials. Some state legislators are content in their positions and have no desire to seek higher office, but many see state and local positions as stepping-stones to national or statewide posts. In the 108th Congress, for example, all but one of the eleven new senators had previously served in elected office. The one exception, Elizabeth Dole, had a strong record of government service, having served as President Reagan's secretary of transportation and President George H. W. Bush's secretary of labor. The career paths of members of the House are more varied, yet even in that chamber forty of the fifty-four newcomers came to Washington in 2002 with experience in elected office.

Hart's win was among a handful of key races that secured a slim majority for the Republicans in the 107th Congress. Politicians and pundits alike viewed the 38-year-old Hart as a rising star in the national party. Describing her selection to deliver the Republican response to Bill Clinton's radio address the Saturday after her big win, the *Almanac of American Politics* noted, "Republican leaders quickly spotlighted their hard-charging newcomer."[3] Representative Jennifer Dunn, then a member of the powerful Ways and Means Committee, praised the freshman congresswoman, telling a reporter the month after Hart's arrival in Congress that "she's going to be in leadership, I can tell you right now. . . . She'll be a very good mesh with the new [George W. Bush] administration."[4]

When Melissa Hart stands up to greet a constituent or lobbyist, her presence is commanding. Nearly six feet tall, with shoulder-length dark brown hair and a wide smile, Hart can work a room with the talent of a skilled, seasoned politician. Perhaps a reflection of her childhood with two older brothers and more than a decade breaking gender barriers in her chosen profession, Hart defies typical feminine stereotypes. A strong and assertive woman, she rarely minces words. Jovial and sarcastic, she is known for her quick and often acerbic wit. Hart speaks her mind, sometimes to her political peril, as friends and foes will attest. She rears back instinctively when someone calls her "Representative Hart"; constituents and lobbyists alike quickly learn that she is simply "Melissa."

At the beginning of the session, Hart received an official-issue Blackberry wireless device to ease instant communication throughout the Capitol complex and on the road. The device fits her lifestyle and personality. Constantly on the go and rarely able to sit still for extended periods of time, she can often be found participating in a meeting while simultaneously working both thumbs to type out yet another quick e-mail reply on the gadget's tiny keypad. In her rare moments of downtime, she enjoys hosting dinner parties highlighted by home-cooked Italian food or playing a round of golf.

ESTABLISHING PRIORITIES IN THE STATE SENATE

Hart championed a wide variety of issues during her decade of service in Harrisburg. Concerned about the burden of taxation and interested in building the economy and creating jobs, her legislative priorities included supporting tax reform (such as successful battles to give voters more control over property taxes and to reduce inheritance taxes), encouraging school choice, providing job and life skills training to domestic violence victims and so-called displaced homemakers, and promoting economic development.

Although Hart focused many of her legislative goals on issues she could address as chair of the Senate Finance Committee, she also pursued legislation to address concerns in other policy areas. Her interest in economic development, taxes, and social security issues runs deep, but perhaps no issue inspires Melissa Hart to action as much as that of abortion. A devout Catholic who believes that life begins at conception, Hart has been a strong advocate for pro-life issues her entire political career. That stance would spell political disaster in many Democratic districts, but Hart's position on this issue is very much in line with most of her constituents. Typically pro-union and liberal on many economic issues, western Pennsylvanians nonetheless are socially conservative and tend to support pro-life candidates.

Hart first learned of Pittsburgh's fledgling safe-havens movement from a constituent letter. Patti Weaver, a Pittsburgh mother and activist, sent Hart a letter describing her work and her concerns about the issue. The letter resonated with the legislator's pro-life commitment, so Hart charged her staff to research how other states were working to support such movements. The result of this research was Pennsylvania's first abandoned-infants bill. On March 21, 2000, Hart introduced S.B. 1346, legislation that would provide a safe haven for babies who might otherwise be left to die. Under its provisions, a parent could relinquish a newborn baby to a hospital, police department, or facility designated as a safe haven without fear of prosecution.

FROM THE STATE LEGISLATURE TO CONGRESS

When Hart left the state senate to assume her post in Washington, S.B. 1346 was still pending, and her commitment to the issue was still strong. High on her list of legislative priorities for her term in Congress was writing a federal bill that would create safe havens for abandoned infants. Doing so would help her develop a reputation as an advocate for women while remaining true to her pro-life beliefs. Safe havens bridge the gap between pro-choice and pro-life legislators by uniting them in support of saving the lives of newborn babies.

One of the classic descriptions of Congress describes the motivation of members of Congress in the starkest of terms, characterizing legislators as "single-minded seekers of reelection."[5] A competing framework for explaining legislative behavior suggests that members of Congress simultaneously pursue two kinds of careers. In their "**constituency careers**," members work in their home districts to secure reelection, responding to the needs of their constituents in order to win votes. But the reelection focus is not enough—successful members must simultaneously pursue "**Washington careers**," working to achieve policy goals and to build power and influence within their chamber. Most elected officials seek office in order to pursue their own political and policy ends. In order to achieve their goals, however, they must first earn the respect of their peers.[6]

When Melissa Hart arrived in Washington to begin her first term in Congress, she pursued both a Washington career and a constituency career. Each weekend she returned to Pittsburgh, working a full schedule in the district, filling the days and evenings with activities such as site visits to local businesses, town meetings, and speaking engagements. In the middle of the week, she attended to her Washington career, trying to build on the legislative accomplishments she had begun in the state senate. When requesting committee assignments, for example, she sought and was given a place on two major committees that would be of particular help in each one of her "careers." The newly created Financial Services Committee had jurisdiction over issues directly related to the financial industry, an important sector in the Pittsburgh area and thus crucial for her constituency career. Service on the Judiciary Committee opened opportunities to build her Washington career. She was named vice chair of the Constitution Subcommittee, the place where most abortion-related bills commence their journey through the House.

Like many other politicians, Hart has taken risks in order to advance her political career. At the end of her first term in the House, Hart made a bold move to strengthen her influence by running for vice chair of the Republican Conference. Although the balloting was far from close—she lost to fifth-term Georgia congressman Jack Kingston by a vote of 159 to 56—outside observers saw her gambit as a sign of future leadership potential. Her appointment to the powerful and prestigious Ways and Means Committee in her third term in office suggests that she is succeeding in building her Washington career.

ESTABLISHING A CONGRESSIONAL OFFICE

The pace in the House of Representatives is too hectic and the workload too vast for any one person to manage alone. As the elected member of Congress, Hart knew that she would set the tone for her office, determine legislative priorities, and make most final decisions. But she also knew that she would need to hire and rely on professional staff to serve as her eyes and ears on Capitol Hill. Successful members know they must delegate authority and responsibility to this team of people who accomplish the day-to-day work of a legislative office. With this in mind, Melissa Hart began assembling a staff for her office in Washington, D.C., and the branch offices scattered around Pennsylvania's fourth district as soon as she won election to the 107th Congress.

Every member of Congress receives an annual representational allowance to pay for the expenses of running an office in Washington and offices in the home district. To keep members from overspending, the statute governing member allowances states that representatives who spend more than their allotment must pay the budget shortfall from their own personal funds. As a result, most member offices run a tight and careful budget. The largest portion of the annual allowance is that for personnel. In the 108th Congress, for example, members were allocated $748,312 to pay the salaries of no more than eighteen full-time employees. The abundant supply of talented and eager workers and a budget constrained by statute means that members need not and do not pay market rates to secure a quality staff.

Congressional staff, as a general rule, are underpaid, overworked, and very young. Descending on Washington each year, hundreds of eager, politically minded young men and women await each opening and fight for the chance to join the ranks of congressional staff. In the offices of particularly irascible members, turnover is high, but new recruits wait in the wings. For example, Congresswoman Sheila Jackson Lee is notorious for her fits of rage in which she sweeps through the office and fires every staff member (save one or two, on rare occasions); as quickly as one group is shown the door, another group enters to start anew.

Hart's view of staff was different: She wanted to assemble a staff of loyal and dedicated workers who would assimilate to her office's culture and stay. During her time in the state senate, she had accomplished this goal. Many staff members in Harrisburg worked for her for years, and several moved from the state senate staff to positions in her various congressional offices.

THE STAFF HIERARCHY

Just as each member brings unique life experiences to the job as legislator, so does each congressional office have its own personality, style, and set of norms. Four different organization structures are most typical on Capitol Hill. Every organization includes staff working in Washington as well as staff located in an office or offices back home, but the chain of command varies. Most House and Senate offices choose a **centralized structure** in which senior staff members report to the chief of staff who, in turn, reports to the senator or representative. A district director (or, in the Senate, the state director) runs the offices in the legislative district but reports to the chief of staff. Much less common is the **Washington/district–state parity structure**. In these offices, Washington staff members report to the chief of staff and district or state office staff report to the district director. The Washington and district offices are equal in authority, and the heads of both offices report directly to the member. The **functional structure,** a third and even less common style, decentralizes authority even further. The head of each office function manages his or her duties and reports to the chief of staff and the member. The final model, **member as manager**, operates in a few House offices but is unrealistic for larger Senate staffs. In such an office, every staff person reports to the member of Congress. Serving as the gatekeeper for all decisions, members typically micromanage office activities.[7]

Hart's office chose a centralized management structure, allowing the chief of staff to serve as the primary gatekeeper for the congresswoman. Although aides have access to Hart and can seek her direct feedback when necessary, she does not involve herself directly in the day-to-day decisions of the office.

Although no two offices are exactly the same, most Washington staffs include the following positions.

The **chief of staff** (sometimes called the administrative assistant) directs the operations of the entire staff, typically including those employees in the district offices. In the absence of the member, this person is the final authority and often has the power to speak directly for his or her boss. In most offices, the chief of staff oversees the other staff members, helps chart the legislative and political agenda of the office, builds and maintains connections important to the member, and serves as a sounding board for the boss. As the most senior person on the staff, he or she is usually well paid. Most chiefs of staff have previous work experience on Capitol Hill or in state politics.

The **legislative director** (LD) is responsible for directing the legislative agenda and helping promote the member's policy priorities. The LD monitors the legislative calendar, keeping track of what bills are coming to the floor and what legislation is moving through committee. The LD oversees the other members of the legislative staff, **legislative assistants**, who are each assigned specific issues. Each legislative assistant (LA) handles his or her issue areas by conducting background research, meeting with constituents and lobbyists, generating ideas for legislation, building support for legislation, and keeping the member apprised of new developments. Many offices assign an LA to each committee on which the member serves; that LA learns about the issues under the committee's jurisdiction, attends committee meetings, and otherwise helps inform and assist the member with his or her committee responsibilities.

The **press secretary**, or director of communications, handles all interaction with the news media. This staff member fields phone calls and e-mails from reporters and cultivates relationships with the media. In many offices the press secretary also serves as a speechwriter, preparing talking points or sometimes entire speeches for the member. Although much of the job is reactive, a good press secretary is also very proactive, suggesting story ideas to reporters that highlight issues the member is working on, scheduling appearances, writing op-eds and press releases, and otherwise generating positive media coverage for the boss.

The **scheduler** sorts through all the invitations the member receives, turning down most requests and accommodating some. Members of Congress work long hours. A typical day begins with an early breakfast meeting, includes committee hearings and constituent meetings throughout the day, and ends late at night or into the early morning hours with a series of votes. The scheduler plans each day, adding appointments to the calendar and managing last-minute changes. Helping the member manage his or her time, the scheduler is the intermediary between the member and the hundreds of people who request appointments in any given week.

An essential staff position in almost any office is the **legislative correspondent** (LC). In most offices, this staff member manages office correspondence, writing and sending responses to the floods of constituent mail that members of Congress receive. If an office does not hire an LC, legislative staff often share responsibility for responding to the mail.

Although not always specific positions, offices typically hire staff to serve as **office manager** and **systems administrator**. The office manager assists with the daily functions of running an office, including payroll, accounts, and other necessary paperwork. The systems administrator is the point person for technology and computing services in the office. In many offices, a staff member with another primary duty will also assume these responsibilities. For example, many schedulers also serve as office managers.

The **staff assistant** serves as the first line of defense for the member and the rest of the staff. He or she sits in the front office, answers the phones, and greets visitors. Although not a particularly glamorous job, the staff assistant position is the typical route of entry to work on Capitol Hill. Few people remain in this job for long; it is almost always a stepping-stone to a higher position within the office or elsewhere on Capitol Hill.

Assembling her Washington team, Hart first hired Bill Ries to be chief of staff. Ries had been Hart's chief of staff in Harrisburg, so he understood not only Pennsylvania politics but also, more important, Melissa Hart—her personality and her brand of legislating. To assist Ries in the Washington office, Hart selected her campaign manager, Christian Marchant, to serve as legislative director. Together, this trio—Hart, Ries, and Marchant—poured over résumés and conducted interviews until they had assembled the Washington team.

In addition to the permanent staff, I was hired as a congressional fellow. A fellow is a temporary, full-time position for someone who leaves a related profession to work on Capitol Hill. After a designated length of time, the fellow returns to his or her profession with a clearer understanding of how Congress works. I was on sabbatical from Franklin and Marshall College in Lancaster, Pennsylvania, and sought the fellowship in order to learn about congressional politics from the inside.

With a staff in place, Hart was ready to begin work as a U.S. congresswoman. Equipped with ten years of state legislative experience and enthusiasm for her new role, Hart and her team set out to chart a course for her first term in the House of Representatives.

CHAPTER SUMMARY

In addition to the major bills that pass through Congress every session and make national headlines, many smaller bills addressing individual issues also pass into law each session. Tracing the path of one of these small bills, this book tells the story of how H.R. 2018, the Safe Havens Support Act, developed from an idea into part of two larger social service bills passed by the U.S. House of Representatives. This chapter began by introducing Representative Melissa Hart, a freshman Republican from Pennsylvania who was the lead sponsor of the Safe Havens Support Act. Next we discussed Congresswoman Hart's policy priorities as a state senator and then as a newly elected member of Congress. Among her top priorities is the abortion issue; Hart has been a consistent advocate for pro-life legislation.

Before Congresswoman Hart could pursue her legislative goals, she needed to set up her congressional office. This chapter introduced four different models of staff hierarchy that members of Congress typically use: centralized structure, parity structure, functional structure, and member as manager. It concluded with a discussion of staff positions common in congressional offices and reviewed Hart's staffing decisions.

NOTES

1. Mackenzie Carpenter, "After Keeping Her Party in Control of the Legislature, She's Set Her Sights on a Congressional Seat," *Pittsburgh Post-Gazette*, October 15, 2000, A19.
2. Ibid.
3. Michael Barone, Richard Cohen, with Charles E. Cook Jr., *The Almanac of American Politics 2002* (Washington, D.C.: National Journal Group, 2001), 1310.
4. Rachel Smolkin, "Hart's Star Rises Quickly in Congress," *Pittsburgh Post-Gazette*, February 4, 2001, A1.
5. David Mayhew first presented this thesis in his influential book *Congress: The Electoral Connection* (New Haven, Conn.: Yale University Press, 1974).
6. Richard Fenno, *Home Style, House Members in Their Districts* (Boston: Little, Brown, 1978).
7. The Congressional Management Foundation, a nonprofit consulting group that provides training and assistance to help congressional offices operate more effectively, describes these management styles in their guide for new members: *Setting Course: A Congressional Management Guide* (Washington, D.C.: Congressional Management Foundation, 2004).

REINVENTING THE WHEEL

CONDUCTING BACKGROUND RESEARCH

On my first day of work, I arrived at the office ready for a new challenge but unclear about my role and duties. After introducing me to the staff and giving me a quick tour of the office, Bill Ries, the chief of staff, directed me to my new work space, a small desk in the front office that was shielded by a bookshelf. The desk was bare, except for an electric pencil sharpener in one corner. Assured that I would have a telephone and a computer "sometime soon," I was told to settle in.

Members of Congress receive office assignments in a process similar to college dormitory room draw. The members join a lottery by the year they entered the chamber and choose new office space—the longest-serving members first, the freshmen last. In succession, returning members decide if they want to stay in their old office space or if they would prefer to switch to one of the offices vacated by former members and those who have selected a new space. Much like the college equivalent, by the time the room selection process reaches the freshman class, the choices are few and the offices small.

For a freshman office, Longworth 1508 was a good space. Near the elevator bank, Hart could quickly maneuver to the Capitol building across the street for the roll-call votes that would inevitably interrupt meetings in the office. Split into three main rooms, the small suite included an office for the congresswoman, a large entry room, and a back office hidden from view. The entrance space, subdivided in the back to create two small offices for senior staff, served multiple purposes, including as a greeting and waiting area, a meeting space, and an open work space for junior-level staff. A side doorway opened to a closet with room for a microwave, a half-sized refrigerator, and one staff desk as well as an open office for four or five desks. This back room became the "ledge shop," the work space for the legislative assistants and the scheduler. The cramped quarters in the back office made me quickly appreciate my desk in the entrance area; the bookshelf offered at least a modicum of privacy for me and my pencil sharpener.

That first afternoon I met with Christian Marchant, the legislative director, for about an hour to discuss the congresswoman's work in the Pennsylvania senate on two bills, one about job training for displaced homemakers and women in transition and the other about safe havens for abandoned infants. Like many people, I had read an occasional newspaper story about a newborn baby found dead in a wooded area or trash dumpster, but I knew nothing about legislative efforts to address the problem. After Marchant's brief introduction, I was charged to learn about the issue, make suggestions to the congresswoman for potential federal legislation, and then write a bill she could introduce and promote. A trained academic researcher but a neophyte in Congress, I knew little about how to transform an idea into a bill.

This chapter examines the process by which members of Congress and their staff learn about issues and research the legislative history of policy ideas, including the general principles that guide background research and several of the resources available to assist congressional staff in this process. All of this will be illustrated by my research on the abandoned-infant problem.

THE IMPORTANCE OF DOING YOUR HOMEWORK

The first step necessary for transforming an idea into a bill is conducting background research. It is quite common for legislative staff to know little or nothing about a specific policy issue when they first begin their work. Even staff who have worked an issue area for years need to update and fine-tune their knowledge. So, before crafting an initial proposal, legislators and their staffs first investigate the scope and extent of the problem they wish to remedy with legislation. At the same time, they determine what, if anything, has already been attempted and accomplished to address this specific concern. If someone has already introduced a bill doing what the legislator wishes to do, why reinvent the wheel?

Any piece of legislation is only as powerful and effective as the depth of understanding that inspires the bill. Without a clear knowledge of past and present legislation on related issues and without systematic research that uncovers the depth and complexity of the policy at hand, no relevant legislation can be developed. Thus, the first step for translating an idea into a bill is thorough research.

LEGISLATIVE HISTORY

The first research phase is to determine what laws already exist and what legislation has been introduced (though not passed) before. Tracking the legislative history of a policy issue serves several important purposes. It details what legislators have already attempted and accomplished, it identifies related bills scheduled for renewal in an upcoming session, and it reveals gaps in existing policy.

When considering introducing a new bill, legislative staff first familiarize themselves with similar laws currently "on the books." An idea may appear novel and inventive to a member or staffer, but another legislator may have already translated the same idea into law. Experts at the Congressional Research Service and on committee staffs follow policy issues carefully and usually know what existing laws relate to an issue and what legislation has been tried but has failed. In addition, policy experts will know what bills are expiring soon and will need **reauthorization**. Many bills that create new programs authorize federal funding for a limited time frame, commonly five years. At the end of the allotted time, the funding expires. If Congress does not act to renew or extend its funding, a program will not receive federal money in the coming fiscal year. Thus, the reauthorization process requires Congress to revisit issues and either renew particular laws or let their programs die.

The Elementary and Secondary Education Act (ESEA), for example, provides federal government funding to assist public schools that meet specific guidelines. Every five years, Congress reconsiders the ESEA and writes new guidelines. If a legislator wants to make changes in federal policy related to elementary education, it is easiest to create new policy by revising the ESEA during its next planned reauthorization. Any member of Congress can introduce an education bill at any time, but timing a bill to coincide with a major education reauthorization increases the likelihood that the bill will move through the legislative process.

Another reason to research legislative history is to find gaps in existing policy. Members of Congress and their staff work hard to create legislation that solves problems and meets needs, but even the most thorough law includes loopholes. Once a law is in effect, the individuals who implement it and those affected by it may discover gaps in its services or other unanticipated results. Legislators routinely write bills called "**technical amendments**" that make small changes to existing law and address these unexpected problems. Because technical amendments are usually uncontroversial and become law with little fanfare, technical amendment packages are another place to introduce a small policy change and maximize the likelihood that the idea will become law.

Besides providing information about current laws in a given policy area, background research will also uncover bills that did not succeed in becoming law. These "unsuccessful" bills sometimes turn out to be the legislative equivalent of buried treasure. Many legislators introduce the same bill Congress after Congress until the timing and political climate ripen so the bill can finally pass. When studying the history of failed legislation, a staff member tries to determine what factor or factors inhibited a bill's passage. Sometimes a bill needs a champion from the committee that has jurisdiction over its subject; sometimes a legislator introduces a bill for symbolic reasons and makes little effort to move it through the legislative process. In still other cases, an otherwise popular bill may contain one controversial provision that impedes its passage. By identifying the reasons previous bills stalled, an entrepreneurial legislator can uncover ways to introduce similar legislation that will have a greater likelihood of passage. Failed legislation sponsored by retired or defeated members is a great source for recycled bills. By searching through the list of bills sponsored by a former member, staff can find old bills to "borrow," edit, and reintroduce.

Just as the history of failed bills may signal new legislative opportunities, this step in the research process also identifies issue and policy areas wrought with political danger. If policy experts identify "red flags" or warn that a particular issue will incite strong negative reactions, a legislator may want to reconsider introducing a particular bill, especially early in his or her career.

Research on safe-havens bills uncovered very few federal efforts to address the issue. In the 106th Congress (1999–2000), the House passed H.Res. 465, a measure that makes an official proposal but requires no action. The resolution "expressing the sense of the House of Representatives that local, State, and Federal governments should collect and disseminate statistics on the number of newborn babies abandoned in public places"[1] passed by voice vote on April 11, 2000. Responding to a wave of infant abandonments in her district, Representative Sheila Jackson Lee introduced H.R. 4222, a bill to create a Bureau of Labor Statistics task force to study infant abandonment and report its findings to Congress. The proposal died in committee in the 106th Congress, so Lee reintroduced the bill as H.R. 71 in the 107th Congress. Like the earlier version, the bill never saw committee action.

THE ART OF POLICY RESEARCH

Research is more an art than a science. Discovering the important facts, sorting out superfluous information, and assembling the best sources requires knowledge, creativity, and a bit of luck. Although it is impossible to create a simple "how-to" list of the steps to faultless policy research, certain core principles guide the most effective legislative research.

IDENTIFYING THE PROBLEM

Often ideas for legislation begin with a legislator's general sense that a problem exists though he or she doesn't have much background information that points toward a solution. Although it is not necessary to grasp the full extent of a concern before deciding to take action, research is an essential first step in understanding the complexities of an issue and determining the best way to address it. Some people do try to create solutions without defining problems first, but it makes far more sense to identify the nature and extent of the policy concern that needs to be addressed before designing a potential solution.

A legislator, constituent, or staff member may have a general sense that a problem exists but not know many details. With some investigation, however, the researcher can begin to pinpoint the nature of the problem and look for means to a public policy solution. By investing the time to determine the likely causes of a problem, legislators can identify the most probable route to a solution and target a response most effectively.

In the earliest stages of researching the abandoned-infants bill, the initial task was defining the problem. Searches of the Lexis-Nexis major newspapers database, for example, uncovered hundreds of stories about the discovery of abandoned babies. In some instances, a bystander heard an infant cry, investigated, and found the baby in time to save his or her life. Most of the news reports were far more grim, detailing the discovery of babies dead from exposure. One story told of an infant discovered dead in an Iowa snowdrift; another told of a dead baby found on the floor of a portable toilet at a Delaware construction site. Information in most of these cases was sketchy at best; the authorities rarely found the person responsible for abandoning a baby, and communities reacted to the grisly discoveries with shock and dismay. The more I researched incidents of infant abandonment, the more aware I became of the lack of concrete data to determine the scope and nature of the problem.

DISCOVERING GAPS IN THE RESEARCH

One of the first things I learned was how little anyone really knows about infant abandonment. As much as everyone working on the topic wants to know how many babies are abandoned each year in the United States, such data are all but impossible to find. Neither the federal government nor most states keep statistics tracking the number of newborns abandoned or how many die each year as a result. Although crime data indicate numbers of infant homicides, states do not distinguish between those babies who die as a result of unsafe abandonment and those who die as victims of other homicides. Mothers of abandoned newborns are women in crisis. Unable or unwilling to care for her infant, such a mother has made the desperate decision that she cannot keep her newborn child. She usually succeeds in hiding her identity, so it is very difficult to learn details about who is most at risk of abandoning a baby and thus how to prevent the crisis that led to the abandonment in the first place.

After conducting several internet searches and looking through various databases of books and articles, I found the work of Michelle Oberman, a law professor whose research included work on infanticide and neonaticide. Encouraged by this discovery, I called Professor Oberman. She sent me her article "Mothers Who Kill" via overnight mail and scheduled a time later in the week for us to discuss her research findings.[2]

The discussion with Oberman offered new insights into the problem of infant abandonment. Although her work analyzed accounts of women discovered and subsequently prosecuted for killing their babies, Oberman's research reveals some of the characteristics of women at risk of abandoning their newborns. Distinguishing cases of neonaticide, killing an infant within 24 hours of its birth, Oberman finds that "the circumstances that surround neonaticides are remarkably consistent and, on the whole, entirely distinguishable from the fact patterns associated with the homicide deaths of older infants and children."[3] Although the race, class, and intellectual ability of these mothers vary, Oberman's comparison of mothers who kill newborns finds many similarities among them. Typically young and single, most of these women live with family but isolate themselves: "An even more fundamental similarity among these cases is the accused woman's seemingly self-imposed silence and isolation during pregnancy. Very few of the accused women told their families and friends that they were pregnant."[4] Scared, disconnected, and often in a state of denial, many of these young mothers face their situation without outside help.

The discussion with Oberman also reinforced the conclusion that it is difficult to measure the scope of the problem. Some abandoned babies are discovered in public places, suggesting that the mother hoped and planned for people to find the child alive and well. But some newborns are discarded in trash bins or secluded areas; occasionally, people discover an infant apparently buried alive. For every bystander who notices something amiss and finds a discarded newborn, countless other abandoned babies likely die without anyone finding the body—or any other evidence of the crime.

When I began searching databases and talking with policy experts to compile estimates of the number of infants abandoned each year, I found that most people cited one study: an unpublished Department of Health and Human Services (HHS) Lexis-Nexis database search of major newspapers that counted 65 published reports of abandoned babies in 1991 and 108 reports in 1998.[5] The HHS "study" was far from a systematic measure of the extent of the problem; indeed, the report itself noted the limitations and weaknesses in the method of its data collection. Opponents of abandoned-infants legislation regularly cited the HHS report as an authoritative source demonstrating the limited scope of the problem.

Clearly, gathering reliable data on the number of abandoned infants and the characteristics of the parents who desert them is difficult, so researchers often rely on news media reports, an admittedly imperfect measure of the problem's scope. Nothing guarantees a newspaper will report every abandoned infant. The discovery of a dead newborn will often make the news, but the discovery of a live infant may not warrant as much attention. On busy news days, either story could get lost. In addition, research that, like the HHS study, is limited to major newspapers participating in a database will capture many in the largest media markets but will miss thousands of other smaller papers that run across the country.

Searching Web sites of safe-havens organizations across the country uncovered anecdotal evidence from the states confirming suspicions that the often-cited HHS report vastly underestimates the actual number of babies abandoned each year. For example, in the twelve months before Texas passed safe-havens legislation, at least thirty three babies were discovered abandoned. According to the Illinois Department of Children and Family Services, thirty two to thirty four infants were found abandoned each year from 1997 to 1999. In southern California, at least fourty five infants were found dead in a 4-year period. Some individual states and localities provided legislators their best numbers of infants known to have been abandoned and left to die, but no government department or other organization collected systematic data to measure the scope of the problem.

Disheartened by the piecemeal nature of most of the data on numbers of babies abandoned each year, I found it even more difficult to locate studies identifying the population of parents who abandon their babies. After many discussions with interest-group staff and searches of Internet databases, I found little concrete data. The only information readily available comes from the few cases when a police investigation leads to the parent or someone confesses to the authorities. Such scanty, anecdotal evidence suggests that mothers who abandon their babies are often young (but not exclusively teenagers) and that many of these women lived with family during their pregnancies. Many of the women apparently hid their pregnancies from loved ones, and in some instances mothers denied the pregnancy even to themselves until the inevitable labor and delivery.

All these research findings convinced me of the need for systematic research and more accurate measures of the scope of the problem. Anecdotal evidence is not sufficient to provide the background and knowledge necessary to design long-term policy. Laws that would help reduce the number of abandoned babies need a foundation in better data.

SETTING REALISTIC RESEARCH GOALS

Although it is very important to conduct research to estimate the scope and scale of a problem, it is equally important to set realistic goals. Public policy issues are complex. Policymakers typically solve the problems that can be easily resolved; the more complex matters, the ones that require significant time, effort, and/or money for future endeavors, are often left in search of solutions. Many of the most pervasive and vexing policy problems have haunted elected officials for decades, their solutions ever elusive.

When examining a complex policy issue, a researcher will continually discover new questions to ask and new avenues for study. The key to quality legislative research is determining how much information is sufficient. Once the research is under way, it becomes easier to identify which information is essential for understanding a policy idea and which information is extremely difficult, if not impossible, to uncover. With limited time and resources, a congressional aide cannot answer every question and follow every lead. Instead, a researcher tries to identify the most important questions and to devote sufficient effort to answering them. He or she focuses attention on gathering the data needed to move to the next step in the process.

LOOKING FOR AREAS OF NEED

Looking into a policy's background, a researcher is on alert for recurring problems, persistent questions that never seem to be answered, or areas where a need seems most immediate or acute. The research process may begin with the goal of addressing one problem, but along the way another problem may arise that seems more urgent or more readily solved through public policy. Keeping an open mind, an attentive researcher can identify new areas of need that may redirect the legislation eventually written and introduced.

As I researched state safe-havens policies, I discovered that states were very quickly passing laws to change or adapt criminal codes so as to encourage the use of designated safe havens and discourage unsafe abandonment of an infant. Such laws were popular and typically passed by significant majorities (for more details on the growth of state safe-havens laws, see chapter 5). However, very few of these state laws included any funding to educate the public about the changes. Every activist and interest group leader I contacted concerning safe-havens programs mentioned the need for money to "get the word out." As they explained, if women in a crisis situation do not know that they have an option to safely relinquish a newborn without criminal penalties, they will continue to abandon babies and place lives at risk. By researching the issue and talking with those most knowledgeable about the abandoned-infants problem, I discovered an area of great need that public policy in most states had yet to address.

IDENTIFYING FRIENDS AND FOES

While doing research, policymakers also begin to identify both potential friends who can help in the legislative process and potential foes who might impede it. Many names will appear and reappear with regularity. For example, if a staff member finds that a certain member of Congress has sponsored or played a key role in most of the related bills researched or if Internet searches consistently link to a particular interest group's press releases and policy alerts, that staff member will probe further. It rarely takes much time before research uncovers a list of "usual suspects"; the natural next step is learning who will likely help and who will likely hinder the new, related legislation.

In most cases, a quick read of a Web site or a review of previously sponsored legislation will clarify an individual or group's position on an issue. Most organizations clearly express and readily share their views. In those cases, however, where their stance seems ambiguous, discrete discussions with trusted insiders will provide the best opportunity to help characterize a group as a likely friend or foe. Particularly in the very early stages of policy development, it is wise to keep a low profile with potential opposition. If background research suggests that a group may not be supportive, it is a better use of energy to save interaction until later in the legislative game.

In the early stages of my research, for example, I discovered the Abandoned Infants Assistance Resource Center (AIARC) at the University of California at Berkeley. Elated to find what appeared to be a research center devoted entirely to the issue, I visited the center's Web site and called to speak with staff members. I soon learned that the AIARC was created as a result of the Abandoned Infants Assistance Act, a law designed to help babies (many of whom were HIV infected and drug addicted) left at the hospital by mothers unable or unwilling to care for them. According to HHS statistics, as many as 30,000 babies nationwide each year are either abandoned at the hospital after their birth or not released to their parents because of concerns about the babies' welfare. When many advocates for these categories of abandoned infants heard that our office wanted to provide federal assistance to another, much smaller category of abandoned infants, they were unhelpful. Likely they feared that the congresswoman wanted to divert some of the money allocated for their cause to a somewhat different purpose; some staff made it clear that they were addressing a problem affecting thousands of babies, whereas our issue affected tens or maybe hundreds of infants each year. On their scale of significance, discarded babies mattered less.

RESOURCES AVAILABLE TO CONGRESSIONAL STAFF

A congressional office has several resources at its disposal to assist with the research process that are especially helpful when trying to understand a new policy issue. Using these resources can save much time and frustration. Many organizations employ people for the sole purpose of conducting background research and packaging it in ways that would be most useful to members of Congress and their staff. Some of the best of these resources are available directly on Capitol Hill.

OTHER STAFF IN THE MEMBER'S OFFICE

The first place to look for ideas and leads when beginning research is inside the member's office. The staff members who have worked longest on Capitol Hill often remember a related bill or legislative battle from past years that might be important to reference. All staff members can suggest people useful to contact, such as helpful lobbyists, particularly friendly staff members in other congressional offices, and committee professional staff who work on related issues. A field representative working in a district office can offer insights on how a proposed policy might impact the district and suggest names of informed local contacts. By talking with others inside the office, a staff member can learn subjective insider information that would be much more difficult to find elsewhere.

When beginning to research the safe-havens issue, the other staff in Hart's office provided helpful suggestions of people to contact. Since the congresswoman was in her first term, the senior staff were not well connected to the Washington community, but they did offer ideas for building connections within Pennsylvania. On advice of the chief of staff, for example, I contacted Scott Malan of the Hospital Association of Pennsylvania. He helped connect me with contacts at the national headquarters of many health care associations.

THE CONGRESSIONAL RESEARCH SERVICE

Created in 1914 as the Legislative Reference Service, the **Congressional Research Service** (CRS) is an agency within the Library of Congress that serves the mission of "providing the Congress, throughout the legislative process, comprehensive and reliable analysis, research and information services that are timely, objective, nonpartisan, and confidential."[6] Members of Congress and their staff can request that a CRS analyst research any topic; in essence, CRS is a building full of Ph.D.s only a phone call away equipped to answer questions, provide background details, and write reports. In the political and often intensely partisan environment of Capitol Hill, CRS serves as an objective source for data and information.

The CRS functions as a resource to congressional staff in several different ways. First, CRS maintains a Web site available only on the congressional intranet with a searchable database of thousands of reports on hundreds of policy issues. The reports vary from short memos to long reports of a hundred pages or more and often provide "one-stop shopping" for the latest data on government programs and legislative initiatives. An attentive reading of a few CRS reports often provides enough background information and policy-related vocabulary to verse even the most novice staffer on an issue and prepare him or her to ask informed questions of outside sources.

In addition to reading the available CRS materials, staff members can also call CRS experts directly to clarify details and ask questions. In general, CRS analysts are highly trained researchers who understand the complexities of policy issues, and they are expected to respond immediately to calls from a congressional office. A phone conversation with an author of a particularly helpful report will usually provide rich details unlikely to appear in published form. Attentive to the goal of providing objective and nonpartisan analysis, CRS analysts exercise caution when writing their reports. In conversation, however, many experts feel comfortable offering their personal impressions of an issue debate and will more easily reveal unofficial "stories behind the story" that help to make sense of hard-to-explain legislative actions.

When working on job-training legislation, for example, I called CRS experts to discuss the Perkins Act. By the end of an hour-long phone conversation, I understood much of the political history of the program and some of the reasons for changes made in the most recent reauthorization of the bill. This conversation provided valuable insider information that helped the congresswoman weigh different options for how to proceed.

Although CRS experts are constantly writing and updating reports on a wide range of issues, any member of Congress or congressional staff can request that CRS answer a specific question or conduct new research. Often an office requests a CRS memorandum on an issue to save valuable staff time; sometimes a staff member will ask the CRS to collect particular data in order to maintain confidentiality. Analysts in the CRS do not reveal the names of the members or offices for whom they are conducting research, a policy that is particularly important when data are politically sensitive. For example, if a vocal pro-life member of Congress wants to know how many teenagers cross state lines to receive abortion services, he or she will almost certainly find abortion clinics unwilling to cooperate with the request. A nonpartisan and issue-neutral CRS expert, in contrast, will encounter less resistance when asking for the same information.

After spending a few days conducting independent research on safe havens, I visited the CRS Web site to download reports about abandoned infants and obtain initial background information. Finding nothing there, I called CRS and asked to speak with an analyst who could answer my questions. Karen Spar, the CRS specialist whose area of expertise was most suited to my subject, promptly returned my call. In this conversation, I learned only that I already knew more about abandoned babies and safe havens than she did. Because safe havens were state laws and not yet the subject of possible federal legislation, CRS had not prepared any background information on them. For most policy issues, CRS will be the single most helpful source of background information and insider accounts of past legislative battles. For this particular issue, however, the subject was too new to Congress and too readily identified as an issue of concern only to the states. I asked Spar to prepare an issue brief on the prevalence of infant abandonment nationwide and make it available to any member of Congress interested in the issue.

As a source of new and solid data, the CRS report was a great disappointment. Spar uncovered most (but not all) of what I had found and unearthed nothing new. In measuring the scope of the problem, the CRS report referenced only one source, the problematic HHS report, and then juxtaposed these HHS numbers with the number of infants abandoned in hospitals, relying on the AIARC, a source with a political interest to protect, for data and explanations. Spar summarized, "Since little is known about the number of infants abandoned or 'discarded' in public places, information also is scarce about the characteristics of these children and their parents, or the circumstances of their abandonment."[7] Finally, the report summarized state activity creating safe-havens laws and noted the few examples of federal legislation that had been introduced in Congress. Learning nothing new, I realized that I would have to look elsewhere for the necessary data.

THE PARTY CAUCUS OR CONFERENCE

Members and senators of each party gather formally in **party caucuses** to plan political strategy and share information. These groups, called the Democratic Caucus and Republican Conference in the House and the Democratic Conference and Republican Conference in the Senate, all maintain Web sites that include party-endorsed information on current legislative issues. Searches of the caucus or conference site will provide a quick gauge of the party's current issue priorities and positions so a researcher can see if an idea for new legislation is a natural complement. In addition, caucuses supply members with legislative summaries and "talking points," lists of snappy comments and prepackaged facts that highlight the party's position on issues of importance to the party. Its leaders maintain separate leadership offices and staffs devoted to helping fellow partisans stay "on message."

COMMITTEE STAFF AND WEB SITES

No individual legislator can be an expert on every issue that comes before Congress in a typical session. Over time, Congress has developed a **committee system** to divide some of the labor and help legislators learn policy details in specific subject areas. Members and senators typically serve on a selection of committees, each with jurisdiction over a particular subject matter.[8]

Each committee and subcommittee hire **professional staff** whose work focuses on specific policies within that committee's jurisdiction. Early in the research process, staff from a member's personal office contact the corresponding committee to find out who on the committee staff works with the policy issue at hand. This staff member will have access to data, background information, and connections to other issue experts. In addition, committee staff will often be the best source for researching legislative history; they can describe what bills will most likely come to the floor in the current session, provide background on related legislation that succeeded or failed in the past, and assess the willingness of the committee to consider a proposed bill.

Staff of the Ways and Means Committee were a helpful resource when researching the safe-havens issue. For example, we met with Matt Weidinger, the staff director of the Human Resources Subcommittee, and staff member Katie Kitchin to learn more about the timing and plan regarding bills scheduled for reauthorization during the 107th Congress. Their subcommittee had jurisdiction over the Promoting Safe and Stable Families Act, the primary federal legislation that funds and directs foster care programs. Since abandoned infants move through the foster care system, we recognized that it might be possible to enfold a safe-havens program within the larger bill.[9]

PRESSING ON TOWARD THE GOAL

With time, common themes began to emerge from the research, although only in the early stages of developing a bill was I aware of several areas of need. All sources lamented the lack of meaningful, scientific data on the extent of the problem and the poor understanding of the risk factors most likely to contribute to infant abandonment. I was coming to the conclusion that any legislative response to the problem of abandoned babies needed to include funding for rigorous data collection. I also became more convinced that federal legislation was necessary. Although state safe-havens laws were passing at rapid speed across the country, the bills lacked consistency from state to state. What was common practice in one state was not allowed in another; federal legislation could help bring much-needed consistency to programs nationwide.

Although the early research raised more questions than it answered, Representative Hart knew that we needed to move beyond researching the issue and focus more directly on creating policy solutions. For that, the next step was to sort through what was within the powers of Congress and what powers should be left to the states.

CHAPTER SUMMARY

Using examples from researching the abandoned-infants issue, this chapter examined the process by which members of Congress and their staff learn about and research policy ideas, including the general principles that guide background research and several of the resources available to assist congressional staff in this process.

The first step in legislative research is gathering background information. Staff members trace the legislative history of policy ideas, looking for similar and related laws already in place as well as bills introduced in previous sessions that did not become law. Successful background research also identifies gaps in existing public policy, generating ideas for proposing new legislation to meet existing needs and correct current problems.

The chapter also outlined the basic steps of policy research beginning with identification of the problem in need of a political solution. After determining the scope of the problem, legislative researchers try to set reasonable policy goals for addressing the issue and to look for areas of need and unanswered questions. Throughout the research phase, congressional staff identify individuals and organizations that will provide assistance while also noting who might oppose policy changes.

Finally, among the many resources available to members of Congress and their aides, one should consider the role of other congressional staff, the Congressional Research Service, political party organizations, and congressional committees.

NOTES

1. HR 465, 106th Congress (accessed at http://thomas.loc.gov/cgi-bin/query/D?c106:2:./temp/~c1063xoYJp::).
2. Michelle Oberman, "Mothers Who Kill: Coming to Terms with Modern American Infanticide," *American Criminal Law Review* 34 (1996): 1–110.
3. Ibid., 22.
4. Ibid., 24.
5. U.S. Department of Health and Human Services, Administration for Children and Families, "Abandoned Babies: Preliminary National Estimates" (accessed at http://www.acf.hhs.gov/news/stats/abandon.htm).
6. Congressional Research Service, "About CRS" (accessed at http://www.loc.gov/crsinfo/whatscrs.html#about).
7. Karen Spar, "'Safe Haven' for Abandoned Infants: Background on the Issue and State Laws," *CRS Report for Congress RS20901*, August 24, 2001, 3.
8. For more details on the role and function of congressional committees, see chapter 8.
9. For additional discussion of Hart's work with the Human Resources Subcommittee staff, see chapter 8.

EDUCATION AND ALLIANCES

WORKING WITH ORGANIZED INTERESTS AND CAUCUSES

Once I began conducting background research on abandoned-infants legislation, the policy options and the issue's vocabulary became more familiar. Having a general idea of what Congress could do to address this concern, it was time to begin drafting some legislative options for the congresswoman to consider. This step begins with networking and building alliances with other people and groups who might have an interest in the policy, in this case, adoption advocates, child welfare professionals, and women's organizations. Outside groups like these would expand my knowledge of the abandoned-infants issue and further prepare me to write a productive bill.

THE IMPORTANCE OF WORKING WITH OUTSIDE GROUPS

Although some staff members choose to work alone when beginning to draft a bill, a "lone ranger" strategy is rarely wise. No legislator can pass a bill alone; passing legislation is, by definition, a team effort. Not only does a member enlist the support and hoped-for votes of other members, but he or she also works to build connections and alliances with interest groups and caucuses that can assist with generating ideas, networking, and preparing a legislative game plan.

Outside groups such as these serve four primary functions in the early phase. Their staffs include experts on a single issue or a set of related issues who can help generate ideas for the details of a bill and can educate the member and his or her staff about specific details that may not have been uncovered in the initial background research. Experienced at following a particular policy issue for many legislative sessions, staff at outside groups can often connect the legislative office with other people who can help build more support for the issue and offer suggestions from their past experiences that will help prepare for political opposition. Every idea will attract at least a few opponents; even a policy that seems as uncontroversial as trying to discourage infant abandonment has its detractors.

This chapter examines two types of organizations that can assist a legislator initiating a new policy: interest groups and caucuses. After describing the general role and function of interest groups, this chapter introduces a few of those that assisted in the development of the Safe Havens Support Act and then discusses the purpose and role of congressional membership organizations, more commonly called caucuses.

THE ROLE AND FUNCTION OF INTEREST GROUPS

At the early stages of developing a bill, organized interests can serve as allies for the congressional staff. At their worst, interest groups can be so narrow and biased as to allow no room for broader public concerns. At their best, they can serve as invaluable sources of information and first links in the chain of support for a proposed bill. In order to maximize the benefits that interest groups offer, however, a lawmaker must take care to understand what these groups do well and how they attempt to achieve their goals.

In its most general sense, an **interest group** is "any group that is based on one or more shared attitudes and makes certain claims upon other groups or organizations in society for the establishment, maintenance, or enhancement of forms of behavior that are implied by the shared attitudes."[1] Two crucial characteristics mark any interest group: (1) a common bond unifies the group (e.g., ethnicity, occupation, ideology, or interest in a particular policy issue), and (2) it takes action to influence public policy in its favor. Legislators often find that working with such groups simplifies responding to people's needs and opens channels of communication. For example, while adoptive parents share a common bond, seeking their assistance on an emergent bill would be an extremely arduous task without an intermediary organization that represents them. Of course, an industrious staff member could begin by calling every adoptive parent he or she knew and asking for their feedback. In researching the Safe Havens Support Act, in fact, we were able to learn about the needs and concerns of adoptive families by contacting an interest group, the National Council for Adoption, to ask about the concerns of its membership. By gathering its members' interests and focusing its efforts, a successful group can provide a helpful service to legislators while advocating policies that benefit its members.

This process of attempting to influence change in legislation is called **lobbying**. An organized interest may try to influence policies directly or indirectly. In legal terms, **direct lobbying** occurs when a paid employee contacts policymakers or their staff members with the goal of influencing government policies[2] or assists with or coordinates others' lobbying efforts.[3] In contrast, **grassroots lobbying** focuses on persuading others to pressure elected officials. Members of Congress will almost always respond to constituents who contact them to express their policy views. Knowing this, interest groups organize campaigns that encourage their membership to write and call their legislators.

Not every group can afford it, but interest groups that have large enough budgets typically maintain an office in Washington, D.C., to track federal policy. Organized interests often find the costs of exercising their "right to petition" the government well worth the expense. The Lobbying Disclosure Act requires that all lobbying firms and all groups that employ in-house lobbyists register with the secretary of the Senate and the clerk of the House of Representatives. Twice a year, the firms must report their spending on lobbying activities. Such record keeping opens the process to public scrutiny so that anyone can track the lobbying activity of groups and their representatives.

Nonprofit associations may also participate in direct or indirect lobbying, but special regulations limit such activity. Federal tax code distinguishes between several types of nonprofits; most political groups organize under either section 501(c)(3) or 501(c)(4) of the Internal Revenue Code. Donors to organizations with **501(c)(3) status** receive tax deductions for their charitable giving. Because of the concerns for potential conflict of interest, these groups generally cannot lobby government officials. Instead, their staff are allowed to provide information that serves to educate—but not influence—a public official. Nonprofit groups that seek **501(c)(4) status** can engage in direct lobbying or campaign activity, but their direct political action comes with a price. Donations to these groups are not tax deductible, making fund-raising more difficult.

In order to maximize donations while maintaining the ability to lobby vigorously, many groups create two distinct organizations with different tax statuses. One organization can offer donors tax benefits but can only "educate" government officials; the other entity within the same nonprofit group can work directly to endorse political candidates and influence legislation, but its donors cannot deduct their contributions.[4] Table 3.1 compares the legal restrictions on the political activity of nonprofit organizations.

An example of an interest group that maintains two different entities is the National Organization for Women (NOW). The original advocacy group with 501(c)(4) status, NOW, boasts half a million members in 550 chapters across the United States. Free to engage in political activity, NOW raises awareness of issues before Congress, organizes petition drives, and encourages members to contact legislators and government officials.[5] The activities of NOW's 501(c)(3) sister organization, the NOW Foundation, are more limited. In order to protect their tax status and offer donors the ability to deduct their contributions, the foundation concentrates its activity on litigation and education, sponsoring conferences, raising awareness of health issues, and providing legal representation in lawsuits defending feminist causes.[6]

TABLE 3.1: SUMMARY OF LOBBYING REGULATIONS FOR NONPROFIT ORGANIZATIONS

TYPE OF NONPROFIT	TAX-EXEMPT STATUS	LOBBYING REGULATIONS (DIRECT AND INDIRECT)

Charitable, religious, or educational organizations	501(c)(3): preferred tax-exempt status	1. Lobbying expenditures must not constitute a "substantial part" of total expenses; OR:
		2. Direct lobbying costs must follow the "expenditure test," limited to:
		  a. 20% of the first $500,000 of total exempt-purpose expenditures of the organization, then
		  b. 15% of the next $500,000 in exempt-purposes expenditures, then
		  c. 10% of the next $500,000 in exempt-purpose expenditures, and then
		  d. 5% of the organization's exempt-purpose expenditures over $1,500,000;
		  e. up to a total expenditure limit of $1,000,000 on lobbying activities.
		  f. Indirect lobbying limits are 25% of the above.

Civic leagues and social welfare organizations	501(c)(4)	1. If the organization receives any federal grant, loan, or award, direct lobbying of federal officials is prohibited. 2. Unless otherwise illegal, direct lobbying of state/local officials and indirect lobbying in general are acceptable under this tax-exempt status, regardless of federal grant, loan, or award.

Donations are tax deductible for the contributor as well.
See 26 U.S.C. § 4911(c)(2).
Jack H. Maskell, "Lobbying Regulations on Non-Profit Organizations," Report for Congress (Washington, D.C., 2002), 5–6.

To encourage support for feminist candidates seeking elected office, NOW is affiliated with two **political action committees** (PACs): the NOW PAC, which raises money for candidates for federal office, and the NOW Equality PAC, which supports state and local office seekers.[7]

Records of official lobbying activity reveal millions of dollars spent each year in an attempt to influence government action. According to data compiled by the Center for Responsive Politics, ideological and single-issue groups reported expenditures of $84,876,808 on lobbying efforts in 2000. The amount of direct lobbying varies greatly. Some groups register lobbyists but report spending no money on such activities. Others devote significant resources to this kind of activity. The Seniors' Coalition, with only four in-house lobbyists, spent more than $9 million in 2000, the Gun Owners of America spent $4.5 million, and the Humane Society reported $1.48 million in lobbying expenditures.[8]

The number and scope of registered lobbyists are quite staggering, with estimates exceeding 12,000 organized interests representing everything from cosmetics to insurance groups.[9] Even though not all these groups lobby Capitol Hill on a consistent basis, the decision to retain professional lobbyists indicates that thousands of organizations stand ready and able to pressure government officials with just a single phone call.

It was all but impossible to determine the number of registered lobbyists that might have an interest in the safe-havens issue. *Washington Representatives*, the authoritative source listing all registered lobbyists, includes 133 organizations advocating for "children and youth" and ninety three groups concerned with law enforcement. A key-word search of another association database identified ninety one organizations concerned with children and adoption. Hundreds of groups with a regular lobbying presence on Capitol Hill had a potential interest in safe-havens laws; the challenge was identifying who would be most likely to work with the office on the bill.

INFORMATION AND EXPERTISE

Interest groups can develop positive working relationships with legislators by providing tools that help simplify the policymaking process. First, because they represent specific populations, interest groups can provide information. As a member of Congress seeks to build and strengthen the case for a potential piece of legislation, a supportive interest group may supply volumes of statistics and studies to bolster arguments in favor of that legislation. Highly regarded interest groups are careful to provide accurate information since their reputations and their successes depend on their truthfulness. If a legislator relies on information from an interest group that later turns out to be false, the group and its representatives will quickly lose their standing on Capitol Hill. Even so, wise lawmakers carefully consider the data and information provided by any outside source, taking care to weed out potential exaggerations and to identify areas of missing information. They also request information and data from multiple sources. Although a careful researcher will always keep in mind that interest-group staff are paid to promote their organizations' interests, working with outside groups to gather information is undoubtedly easier and more effective than researching a new field all alone.

When tracking the explosion of safe-havens legislation in the states, I found that some interest groups were up to date on the issue but that many others distributed outdated information. One pro-life organization, for example, sent us their internal research on safe-havens policies, but all the information was at least a year out of date. In contrast, the most updated information on state abandoned-infants legislation came from the Alan Guttmacher Institute, the independent organization widely recognized as the research arm of Planned Parenthood. Although on the record as skeptical about the effectiveness of and need for safe-havens laws, their information on state infant-abandonment laws was precise, straightforward, and up to date. The best single source of data I found, their "State Policies in Brief" memo, explained the background of the laws and listed the basic provisions and number of laws in effect and currently pending.

Beyond facts and figures, interest groups also provide expert knowledge of issues. Although it is important to collect data to bolster support for legislation, it is equally beneficial to learn from the experiences of interest groups in the policy process. Policy staff members at an interest group can help explain the history of legislation relevant to the group's cause. In addition, because interest-group leaders and staff members regularly attend conferences and meet with individuals and groups to discuss policy and its impact, they have often designed policy innovations and are just waiting for an interested legislator to implement them.

Interest-group leaders typically welcome a call from a congressional office and often provide assistance. For example, when planning the abandoned-infants bill, I called the National Council for Adoption. The response was quick and enthusiastic. Within less than an hour of the original contact, the organization's president, Patrick Purtill, returned my call from his cell phone while traveling in Florida. He expressed his delight in hearing from our office and suggested we schedule a meeting immediately on his return.

The following week, we met for almost two hours. Once we had established that his organization shared fundamental goals and beliefs with the congresswoman, the conversation became open and candid, and I felt free to ask any question. Purtill provided invaluable background information, suggesting names of people and organizations that would likely work with the office and warning where opposition was already beginning to build. For example, Purtill was the first person to send a warning about an organization called Bastard Nation that was actively lobbying against safe havens. The conversation also introduced Representative Hart's staff to new policy ideas. Although aware of the concern that safe-havens programs do not protect fathers' rights, we had yet to learn about a safeguard called putative father registries, which are state programs that allow men who think they might be the father of a child to register their possible paternity and thus safeguard their parental rights. By the end of that meeting, we had enlarged my abandoned-infants vocabulary, gained an important ally in our work, and compiled a list of practical suggestions for ways the federal government might help address the problem of infant abandonment.

NETWORKS FOR MOBILIZING SUPPORT

Besides providing information and expertise to congressional staff, interest groups also tout their networking capability. In many cases, organized interests can mobilize support for (or against) an idea both among the grassroots and on Capitol Hill. Especially with the rise of computer technology, many interest groups can, using e-mail, fax, or phone databases, alert their members instantly about an upcoming bill or committee action and call on them to respond. The National Rifle Association, for example, once claimed that its membership "could generate a half million letters to Congress within three days."[10] A congressional office could not generate this level of response without the aid of an organized interest.

Groups are most effective mobilizing the grassroots when a bill is expected to be on the House or Senate floor for a vote. Concerned interest-group members may flood House and Senate offices with thousands of phone calls and faxes, jamming phone lines and disrupting the offices' work. The Safe Havens Support Act did not get to either chamber for a recorded vote as a stand-alone bill, so Hart's office did not work with many outside groups to energize grassroots pressure on legislators.

In addition, interest groups can help members of Congress build and work with **coalitions**. Most organized interests regularly cooperate with other like-minded groups. As a coalition, groups can pool resources and ideas, sometimes working more efficiently to promote a policy. Some of the most successful interest-group coalitions bring group representatives together to develop a coordinated strategy for mobilizing grassroots pressure. Consider a 5,000-member group that opposes a bill pending in the House. Working alone, such a group will likely have little influence raising its concerns with members of Congress. If, however, the 5,000-member group joins a coalition of other organizations that together represent more than 100,000 members, their coordinated communication campaign could flood members' offices with phone calls, e-mails, and faxes, making a much more noticeable impact.

Staff members from groups that work effectively in coalitions can help connect a congressional member with other organizations that may provide even more information and expertise. In addition, they can link legislative staff with the outreach and lobbying strategists of their coalition. As one contact leads to another contact, an industrious legislative aide can quickly build a network of groups that may assist the office in several stages of the legislative process.

Besides activating the grassroots on behalf of a policy, the right group or set of groups may be able to facilitate support on Capitol Hill when it would be difficult for a member of Congress, working alone, to do so. Some of the largest organized interests have worked on legislation for many decades, so they know which members and staff are most likely to support or oppose a new idea. Such networking is especially helpful for a freshman member who is new to the chamber. In addition, in an era of increased partisanship when fewer legislators are able to build coalitions across party lines, an interest group that has built relationships with many legislators can provide crucial help for bringing members of the other party on board with an idea.

In short, interest groups are experts at promoting their cause within established channels of communication and thus are potent allies. With a single phone call, congressional staff members may save themselves hours of research and dozens of requests for support—a most welcome opportunity in an office of overworked and underpaid legislative assistants.

CAN WE ALL GET ALONG? ANTICIPATING OPPOSITION

Not every interest group will join actively to support a bill, and those with opposing views may become formidable foes if they perceive a threat to their cause. Some groups will naturally oppose certain issue positions. Shrewd legislators and their aides will research potential sources of opposition, familiarize themselves with the group's tactics, and prepare counterarguments if and when opponents attack. If an interest group is fundamentally opposed to a policy idea, it rarely makes sense to solicit that group's assistance.

DISCOVERING ACTIVE OPPOSITION

On its face, the abandoned-infants issue seems uncontroversial: who wants to see an infant left to die in a trash dumpster? In the politics of organized interests, however, one can find a group on both sides of almost any issue.

Overall, support for safe-havens programs was broad and bipartisan. Some groups expressed more enthusiasm than others, but most were either in favor of the policy or neutral. Yet a few organized interests did have reservations about safe-havens laws. Advocates for fathers' rights noted that safe-havens laws rarely address the rights of an infant's father; when a mother in crisis abandons an infant anonymously and turns him or her over to the state, shouldn't the father have a right to claim his child? Early safe-havens laws passed in the states did not address this concern; later versions usually took greater care to protect and preserve fathers' rights. In addition, interest groups advocating open adoptions opposed the anonymity provisions of safe-havens laws, noting that mothers could legally abandon children without providing any medical or family history. Again, later safe-havens laws sought to alleviate

Updated laws tried to alleviate these problems

these concerns by allowing the mother to remain anonymous yet still provide that vital family medical history.

One organized interest comprised of adult adoptees actively opposed all efforts to create safe havens. Known for their "in your face" tactics and brash rhetoric, Bastard Nation raised strong and loud opposition to safe-havens policies. Its representatives testified in legislative hearings, and they were often credited with defeating safe-havens legislation in the few states where it failed.

Neither Hot nor Cold: Working with Critics

Whenever possible, it is best to try to neutralize the opposition. If a group's representatives do not actively oppose a policy proposal but instead appear somewhat skeptical or raise some questions about specific details, it may be wise to include them in the process of creating policy. By interacting directly with them, a legislative office can placate the group's fears and provide the organization a channel for offering its point of view. Even if the potential opponent is unhappy with the final outcome, the group's staff will have a better understanding of the legislator's reasons for proposing a policy and will likely appreciate the opportunity to voice their concerns. Ideally, a congressional office wants to build as broad of coalition of support as possible. With groups that raise concerns about a policy, however, simply convincing them to remain neutral is a great victory.

The Child Welfare League of America (CWLA) had significant concerns about safe-havens programs. The CWLA is a membership organization of public and private child welfare agencies with the stated mission of "engaging people everywhere in promoting the well-being of children, youth, and their families, and protecting every child from harm."[11]

Some of my earliest Internet research pointed me to a panel on abandoned infants that was scheduled during a CWLA national conference held in Washington, D.C., soon after my arrival. In that panel, lasting less than two hours, I learned the latest information on state efforts to fight infant abandonment and made connections with staff from several organizations working on this issue who armed me with brochures, handouts, a video, and a cardboard tube of posters.

A few weeks after the conference, I met with Lupe Hittle, Barbara Allen, and Monica Chopra from the CWLA. Not unsympathetic to the reasons for creating safe havens, the CWLA staff had many reservations about the implementation and overall effectiveness of such programs. Although by no means a guaranteed ally of a federal safe-havens bill, this organization had nonetheless demonstrated an interest in the issue and might be persuaded to support our bill. At a minimum, including them in the conversation would increase our office's understanding of the complexities of the issue and would build a positive working relationship with them.

As representatives of child welfare professionals, the women conveyed some of their concerns and updated me on their work. I learned that the CWLA had invested a significant amount of time in the abandoned-infants issue, including convening a conference devoted specifically to this subject in October 2000. At that conference, they reported results of a survey they had conducted that documented the lack of information and coordination of current work on the abandoned-infants problem. After identifying points of mutual interest and concern, we agreed to share information and help one another collect data on state abandoned-infants laws.

We then turned the discussion to brainstorming about what federal abandoned-infants legislation might look like. The CWLA suggested several items that they believed should be included in a safe-havens bill. In particular, legislation should include funding for research to help identify the scope of the problem, understand more about women who abandon their infants, and evaluate the various safe-havens programs already in place. In addition, the bill should provide "**technical assistance**" to states; that is, the legislation should fund training programs and informational materials to assist states in trying to implement safe-havens laws. The definitions section of the bill was also important to them; definitions of key variables, such as the age of an eligible infant and the facilities that qualify as "safe havens," vary significantly from state to state. Federal legislation that defined terms clearly would be a good first step toward nationwide consistency and would help set national standards.

The conversation also included a dialogue about items that should not be included in a bill. Congress has little constitutional authority to create a national safe-havens policy that exempts parents from criminal prosecution since the states have most authority over criminal law, prosecution, and child welfare agencies. Moreover, the CWLA encouraged Hart to keep the issue of pregnancy prevention and sexuality education separate from legislation assisting safe havens. It would be wise, they counseled, to focus attention first on areas of greatest agreement and avoid these political "hot buttons."

We discussed which interest groups might be willing to help on this bill. Physician groups, adoption groups, pro-life organizations, practitioners dealing with safe havens in their states (e.g., county attorneys and state legislators), private health care and child welfare groups, and some education groups (PTA, school administrators, and college administrators) came to mind.

Lupe Hittle, who had been following the issue from its beginning, noted that opposition to safe-havens bills was beginning to build. In general, she explained, opposition centers around privacy issues, fathers' rights, and lack of information about the infants' medical and family histories. The political right in some states generates opposition by suggesting that these bills encourage irresponsible behavior.

By the end of this meeting, I knew much of what should and should not be written into a federal safe-havens bill. In addition, I had begun to identify

3 main issues

other groups that might work with our office and those that might generate opposition. Building an alliance with this organization was an essential step in writing a broadly acceptable bill.

THE IMPORTANCE OF POLITICAL TIMING

Because organizations have limited time and resources, they cannot work on every issue before Congress in a given session. In the first session of the 107th Congress, for example, members of the House and Senate introduced more than 5,500 bills.[12] Clearly, the most successful interest groups set priorities and target their work to support or oppose a manageable number of bills on a few issues in order to maximize their effectiveness.

Groups varied in their interest in and enthusiasm for Hart's work on the abandoned-infants issue. Some groups expressed mild awareness and eventually offered letters of support. Others expressed little concern at all. For instance, women's groups backed away from safe havens. We introduced the safe-havens idea in a meeting with representatives of the American Association of University Women (AAUW), an organization that describes itself as "the nation's leading voice promoting education and equity for women and girls,"[13] but they did not want to help with the bill. The AAUW, like many national women's organizations, strongly affirms abortion rights, so a bill addressing failed family planning does not fit well with their larger goal of promoting reproductive freedom.

Other groups appeared distracted. Although the issue seemed to line up with the goals of the National Right to Life Committee (NRLC), for example, our office found it nearly impossible to get their staff to return our phone calls. Much of our work on safe havens overlapped with the battle to defeat the McCain–Feingold campaign finance reform bill, a proposal that places restrictions on interest groups. That issue had captured the attention of the NRLC's legislative director, Douglas Johnson; since it was his first legislative priority, he gave it organization time and resources that might have otherwise gone to safe havens.

THE ROLE OF CONGRESSIONAL CAUCUSES

Just as interest groups serve many useful purposes when developing legislation, so also do informal groups of congressmen and women become important resources for building alliances. Within Congress, many members have mutual concerns or share a belief that leads them to work naturally together. While this is expected among colleagues, in most lines of work such affinities might not amount to more than drinks after work on Friday. For lawmakers, however, common ties (ideological, regional, and even athletic) can provide a foundation for collaboration during the legislative process. Members who play basketball regularly in the House gym or who gather for a weekly Bible study make personal connections and friendships that sometimes lead to cooperation on a policy idea. In addition, these informal groups can help members learn about upcoming legislation, think through effective public policy, or improve their performance in the Congress.[14] Over time, some of these unofficial partnerships may mature and evolve into more structured groups with regular meeting times and definable membership boundaries; when they do, these groups are called "**caucuses**." Although voluntary and outside the formal legislative structure, congressional caucuses play an important role in shaping politics and policy on Capitol Hill.[15]

Beginning with legislative reorganizations in the 1970s, Congress recognized structured caucuses called **legislative service organizations** (LSOs) that often held prominent status in the policymaking process. Unlike more casual groups of members who interacted informally, LSOs were given offices on Capitol Hill and employed their own staffs. Many LSOs assessed membership fees, sold publications, and relied on members to donate unused office-expense funds to pay for their operations. Under these parameters, LSOs were essentially housed, staffed, and budgeted by Congress.[16] Examples of influential LSOs included the liberal Congressional Black Caucus, the slightly more moderate Democratic Study Group, and the conservative Republican Study Committee.

In the 104th Congress (1995–1996), the newly installed majority Republican leadership abolished LSOs as part of their Contract with America reforms. Because these groups could use public dollars to fund large staffs, conduct "public forums" that served the same purpose as committee hearings, and design long-term policy agendas, Republicans worried that LSOs were duplicating the work that committees should do. Instead of devoting so much time to writing legislation, they argued, committees should be the primary source of policy development and expertise. LSOs, in effect, created additional centers of power in Congress through which members could circumvent traditional party and committee leadership structures. Although these groups could not accept private money, many LSOs circumvented this rule by establishing separate, related nonprofit entities that could receive money from outside interests and corporations.

Some commentators suggest that the move to abolish LSOs was in part a calculated maneuver on the part of Republicans to weaken opposition and consolidate power. At the time the Republicans regained control of Congress, more LSOs advanced Democratic interests than helped conservative causes.

Regardless of the reasons for eliminating LSOs, congressional Republican leadership quickly discovered that their members enjoyed many benefits from their participation in caucuses. In the first few months of the 104th Congress, the leadership debated whether to allow caucuses in any form; the pressure grew to restore many of the activities previously performed by LSOs. In response, the leadership created **congressional membership organizations** (CMOs) that served many of the functions of the former LSOs but with a few new safeguards. Most of the former LSOs reorganized as CMOs and continued under the same name.

No longer able to work in separate, publicly funded office space like the former LSOs, the new CMOs maintain a presence on Capitol Hill by affiliating with the offices and staffs of their respective members. Each congressional session, the member who chairs a caucus provides office space and sometimes an aide to run the daily activities of that CMO. Despite these opportunity costs, CMOs usually count on a steady membership that finds participation valuable because of the inside information and social connections such groups offer.[17]

Because of the informal nature of some CMOs, it is difficult to know the exact number of caucuses currently active in Congress. The House of Representatives Web site listed 161 CMOS in the 108th Congress (2003–2004), but the actual number is clearly higher.[18] These groups vary widely in size, scope, and significance. Some caucuses form with a defined task, such as the Lewis and Clark Bicentennial Congressional Caucus convened to raise the profile of commemorative events from 2003 through 2006, or the End of the Death Tax Caucus, to build support for repealing estate taxes. Others, such as the House Potato Caucus and the Kashmir Forum, represent regional, ethnic, or affinity groups. Many of the former LSOs that reorganized under the new rules champion particular issues. The bipartisan Congressional Caucus for Women's Issues, for example, alerts its members to legislative developments and encourages cooperation on a range of policies that affect women, but it deliberately excludes the divisive abortion issue. To work with other like-minded members on abortion, the Women's Caucus encourages its members to join either the Congressional Pro-Life Caucus or the Congressional Pro-Choice Caucus.

Melissa Hart's office worked with many caucuses to generate ideas and help build support for abandoned-infants legislation. Parallel to our experience working with organized interests, we found some natural points of connection with like-minded CMOs that could help us move forward with a bill.

The Congressional Pro-Life Caucus, for example, offered enthusiastic support from the very beginning. Caucus staff member John Cusey sent several e-mails encouraging caucus members to support the bill, and many did become cosponsors. The Congressional Caucus for Women's Issues was another helpful CMO. A bill to protect infants from abandonment fit well with the broader goals of that bipartisan caucus, the members of which include many pro-choice and a few pro-life members. The Women's Caucus held weekly staff meetings and much less frequent member meetings, so I distributed information about the Safe Havens Support Act to the caucus staff and added a handful of members to the bill. In addition, many members of the Congressional Black Caucus joined us at the urging of caucus member (and primary Democratic cosponsor) Representative Stephanie Tubbs-Jones.

With support for a safe-havens proposal building with the help of these and other caucuses and interest groups, our office was ready for the next step: writing the bill itself.

CHAPTER SUMMARY

The image of the Lone Ranger enjoys a place of respect in the American psyche. Whether an inventor, an athlete, an artist, or an entrepreneur, we applaud the one who insistently works alone. The member of Congress who wants to author and pass legislation will find that the Lone Ranger approach rarely, if ever, works. Every successful legislator relies on the help of many others, especially interest groups and caucuses.

A group organized to promote a particular issue or set of issues not only can supply a member of Congress with valuable information and research; it can also provide the perspective gained from long experience working with the legislative process. An interest group will know what legislation has been tried before, why it did or did not succeed, and what opposition to expect.

Congressional members find help from each other as well, not only through individual friendships but also through the collective resources of caucuses. Although voluntary and outside the legislative structure, these loose associations of members offer the benefits of collective information, experience, and savvy—not to mention support for a final vote.

NOTES

1. David Truman, *The Governmental Process* (New York: Knopf, 1971), 33.
2. 2 U.S.C. § 1602(8).
3. 2 U.S.C. § 1602(7).
4. Jack H. Maskell, "Lobbying Regulations on Non-Profit Organizations," *CRS Report for Congress RL31126*, September 2001, 3.
5. National Organization for Women, "Information about NOW" (accessed at http://www.now.org/organization/info.html).
6. National Organization for Women Foundation, "NOW Foundation, Inc." (accessed at http://www.nowfoundation.org/).
7. National Organization for Women Political Action Committees, "NOW PACs" (accessed at http://www.nowpacs.org/facts.htm).
8. Center for Responsive Politics, "Lobbyist Spending: Ideology/Single Issue" (accessed at http://www.opensecrets.org/lobbyists/indus.asp?Ind=Q).
9. Number of registrants since April 1, 2000 (accessed at http://www.influence.biz/).
10. Ronald J. Hrebenar, *Interest Group Politics in America* (New York: M. E. Sharpe, 1997), 158.
11. Child Welfare League of America (accessed at http://www.cwla.org/).
12. "Final Resume of Congressional Activity," *Congressional Record-Daily Digest*, May 6, 2003 (accessed at http://thomas.loc.gov/home/resume/107-1res.pdf).

13. American Association of University Women (accessed at http://www.aauw.org/about/index.cfm).
14. For a more complete discussion of the policymaking functions of informal groups, see Arthur G. Stevens et al., "U.S. Congressional Structure and Representation: The Role of Informal Groups," *Legislative Studies Quarterly* 6, no. 3 (August 1981): 415–37.
15. Susan Webb Hammond, *Congressional Caucuses in National Policy Making* (Baltimore: The Johns Hopkins University Press, 2001).
16. Paul S. Rundquist and Lorriane H. Tong, "House Administrative Reorganization: 104th Congress," *CRS Report for Congress*, September 13, 1996 (accessed at http://www.house.gov/rules/96-764.htm).
17. Irwin N. Gertzog, *Congressional Women* (Westport, Conn.: Praeger, 1995).
18. For one representative list, see http://www.house.gov/cha/CMOlist—108th.htm.

POWER TO THE PEOPLE

LEARNING FROM THE GRASSROOTS

With Christopher Upham

During the early stages of researching and writing the Safe Havens Support Act, Representative Hart's office relied on interest groups and caucuses to provide background information and to build networks of support for possible legislation. But national organizations were not the only groups that inspired the new bill. Just as Hart first learned about the issue from an activist constituent, so too were other local organizations raising awareness and building support for safe-havens laws. Indeed, the national safe-havens movement does not have its origins in the legislative realm. It began instead with the work and dedication of a few individuals scattered across the country, people who were moved to action by the tragic deaths of newborns in their communities.

After briefly summarizing some of the theory that explains the importance of grassroots involvement in policymaking efforts, this chapter discusses the role of local activists in the creation of national safe-havens legislation, examining case studies of some of the first grassroots organizations created to address the tragic abandonment of infants. These three projects originated in unique circumstances particular to individuals who responded creatively when they realized a problem. What these groups and many similar organizations across the country have in common is their desire to meet the challenge of infant abandonment through creative solutions and novel approaches. Following an account of their origins, contributions, and successes in alleviating the outbreaks of neonaticide, this chapter considers some of the benefits of and drawbacks to working with grassroots activists.

THE ROLE OF GRASSROOTS ACTIVISM

From the Greensboro sit-ins of the civil rights movement to the opposition to President Reagan's cuts in Social Security spending by the American Association of Retired Persons, grassroots activism has played a major role in the direction of public policy and legislation in the United States. Yet in order to understand this phenomenon, one must first ask the question, What is a grassroots campaign? A traditional dictionary definition would describe grassroots as "the groundwork or source of something" or as "people or society at a local level rather than at the center of major political activity."[1] **Grassroots movements** essentially begin with individuals who seek to enact broad social or political change. In addition, since grassroots interest groups are dependent on the contributions of individual members rather than on outside financial contributions or tax revenues, they are granted, by many, a higher level of legitimacy.[2] Outsiders often perceive the efforts of grassroots activists as motivated by concern for the public good rather than mere interest in the well-being of financial backers.

While influencing public policy may be the most immediate concern for most interest groups, it would be a mistake to focus only on effecting changes within circles of elite lawmakers. After all, the general public is the ultimate recipient of any policy changes, for good or ill. Interest group leaders therefore try to work at two levels, sometimes focusing on persuading legislators directly, other times directing constituents to pressure their elected officials. Although it is necessary to influence legislators in order to achieve desired policy goals, in the long run the interests of the people determine the success or failure of policy programs.

Historically, **citizen groups** such as Kiwanis, the Lions, and the American Legion formed around a shared sense of community, and only rarely would these associations enter the policy process. Yet "the rise of a very large, highly educated upper middle class in which 'expert' professionals are prominent along with businesspeople and managers" has changed the context in which interest groups attempt to fulfill their twofold function.[3] In today's fast-paced and affluent society, the average citizen has little free time to give to a community organization but is capable of contributing some money to promote a valued cause. Thus, many membership associations have been transformed into advocacy interest groups that, if they have members at all, do not rely on citizen participation for most or all of their efforts. Instead of investing time and volunteer efforts to support a favorite issue, many Americans are now **"checkbook members"** of interest groups, writing a check to promote the cause and leaving the work of lobbying to professionals. This creates a "top-heavy" civic world in which highly trained professional advocates maintain a strong influence over public policy debates while the general public may have limited and indirect impact.

The elitism of current organized interests has a twofold weakness in a political system where government officials are accountable to their constituencies. First, when control over policymaking rests with a select group of Washington insiders, the general public may easily become estranged from and disillusioned by the process.[4] Second, elected officials may question the extent to which the voters themselves are concerned about an issue brought to the forefront by elite advocates. Consequently, in an attempt to reconnect the constituent and the elected official, elite advocacy groups may solicit help from the grassroots, encouraging constituents to contact their members of Congress to add political pressure. Activating the grassroots helps demonstrate the importance of the issue among voters, providing vital information to a member of Congress:

> Policymakers want to know what proportion of constituents, when voting in the next election, will weigh the actions of their elected representatives on a particular policy issue. More salient policy issues will weigh more heavily on voting decisions than will less salient policy issues, and policymakers rely to a considerable extent on interest groups for current information on which issues rank high on salience.[5]

Grassroots involvement in a policy debate can also increase public awareness of and interest in an issue outside Washington. Once people learn that infants are abandoned and left to die but that legislators could be doing something about the problem, they will be more likely to hold their representatives accountable on the issue. Thus, grassroots activism has influence both inside and outside the Washington beltway, linking elite policymakers to voters and placing the power of special interests back in the hands and hearts of constituents.

ABANDONED INFANTS AT THE GRASSROOTS

Beginning in the 1990s, several grassroots organizations brought the issue of infant abandonment to the forefront of public debate and helped spark a nationwide movement favoring safe-havens legislation at the state level. By presenting profiles of two organizations at the forefront of the grassroots efforts to save abandoned infants, this section traces the origins of these groups, describe their grassroots experience, and evaluate their efforts to increase public awareness and encourage legislative responses to the issue of infant abandonment.

A SECRET SAFE PLACE FOR NEWBORNS

In 1998, television journalist Jodi Brooks of WPMI-TV in Mobile, Alabama, reported on a murder trial in Atlanta, Georgia. The defendants in the case, Mitzi Variali and her mother Diane, were charged with and convicted of drowning Mitzi's newborn son in a toilet.[6] For Brooks, this disturbing incident was not an isolated event: she had recently encountered several similar stories and had reported on multiple infant abandonments along the Gulf Coast.

While this problem appeared to be recurrent and widespread, Brooks could not find anyone actively working to prevent the needless deaths of unwanted babies. For this reason, she took it on herself to find an alternative for mothers in crisis so they would not make the tragic decision to kill their newborns. Brooks envisioned a way for them to relinquish their babies safely without publicizing their pregnancy or fearing legal prosecution.

Brooks's first course of action was to contact the local district attorney, John Tyson, in order to secure his cooperation with her efforts. He agreed not to press charges against women who relinquished their infants on three conditions. First, the mothers should take their babies to any hospital operating in either Mobile County or Baldwin County, Alabama. Second, the infant could be no more than seventy two hours old. Finally, the baby must be delivered to the hospital unharmed. Having secured the support of the judicial system, Brooks's next step was to convince local hospitals to protect the anonymity of desperate mothers who wanted to relinquish their children safely. Believing that this policy would ultimately save the lives of innocent babies, many of the local hospitals consented to become "A Secret Safe Place for Newborns," the name Brooks gave to her program. By November 1998, without the need for legislation or public funding, Brooks had successfully launched an unprecedented program that began to circumvent the deaths of unwanted children.[7]

Once mothers in crisis had an alternative to abandonment, Brooks could proceed to educate the public about this option while also promoting the expansion of her safe-havens program into state law. To accomplish these publicity objectives, the program published a Web site, http://www.secretsafeplace.org, accompanied by a help line to answer questions from distressed mothers. In addition, as a news reporter, Brooks had an ideal venue for spreading the word about safe havens; she campaigned for the program as she traveled, chatted online with viewers of CourtTV after the airing of the Crime Stories episode "Abandoned at Birth," and convinced WMPI-TV, her news station, to air thirty five to forty public service announcements per week. As she traveled around the country, she even testified before state legislatures, urging them to adopt safe-havens programs.[8]

With the help of Brooks's publicity endeavors, "A Secret Safe Place for Newborns" became a success in terms of both its effectiveness and its popularity. As of April 9, 2003, nearly five years after the program's inauguration, seven babies were safely relinquished in Mobile, and no newborns were abandoned to their deaths.[9] With an average of fewer than two infants abandoned each year, this program does not appear to encourage irresponsibility. Furthermore, as critics raised specific concerns about the program, the program responded with new procedures for relinquishing newborns, regulations that would safeguard against potential abuses and dangers. For example, if a mother changes her mind, she has a sixty-day period in which to reclaim the child. As a precaution in the event that the person who dropped off the baby was not authorized to do so, Alabama hospitals notify the public after each infant has been relinquished so that kidnapped babies may be reconnected with their parents. To ensure that reclamation is legitimate, DNA tests confirm the parenthood of the claimant before a child is returned. In addition, the program now provides an information packet to relinquishing mothers that explains what will happen to their child and allows them to send an anonymous medical history to hospitals.[10]

Encouraged in large part by the efforts in Mobile, the Alabama legislature passed a bill in May 2000 creating safe havens statewide.[11] Even though "A Secret Safe Place for Newborns" is still a work in progress, states have used the Mobile program as a model for safe-havens programs and laws throughout the country.

The initial results from Brooks's novel idea suggest that safe havens effectively reduce the number of infant abandonment deaths and demonstrate that the initiative and activism of a concerned reporter and a determined district attorney can make a difference. Despite the possibility of undesirable repercussions from safe-havens legislation, states have deemed it most important to save the lives of babies at risk. As Mobile district attorney John Tyson stresses, "It's a question of balance. And we think in this instance, the more urgent duty is to try to save the life of the child first. Once you have the child safe, you can sort out the other issues."[12] With this as a guiding principle and with Brooks's tenacious grassroots activism, "A Secret Safe Place for Newborns" achieved success in Alabama and became a model for other states as well.

A.M.T. CHILDREN OF HOPE

Timothy Jaccard, an ambulance medical technician (AMT) in Nassau County, Long Island, is another activist who was not content to ignore the issue of abandoned infants. A police ambulance paramedic for more than twenty five years and a Catholic, Jaccard is well known among coworkers for his generosity and selflessness.[13] For him, as for Jodi Brooks in Mobile, the problem of infant abandonment became a concern after he was alerted to the discovery of a dead newborn in a toilet. While working morgue detail in July 1997, Jaccard received a call to remove the remains of a full-term baby girl from a bathroom stall in the district court at Hempstead. When he encountered this dismal scene, he was moved to tears and to action. Rather than leave this unclaimed child to be forgotten, Jaccard resolved to provide a decent burial for Baby Angelica—the name given to the baby by a police officer in Hempstead. After the police finished investigating the homicide (to no avail), Jaccard initiated the process of adopting Angelica and arranged a funeral and burial for her. As he explained, he wanted to provide her with "the dignity and identity that every human being deserves."[14]

Although he did not know it at the time, this would not be the last time Jaccard would initiate the task of adopting a child, only to bury her. Months after Angelica's funeral, Jaccard answered another call to retrieve a discarded newborn, this time discovered in a plastic bag tossed into some bushes. As with Angelica, Jaccard was moved and disturbed by the tragedy of this abandoned child. What is more, he believed that these cases were reaching him for a reason, perhaps as a sign from God. So, combining his recent experience of adopting and burying an abandoned child with his twenty five years worth of connections in the Nassau County Police Department, Jaccard sought volunteers and support for his cause. The result was the creation of a nonprofit organization called the "A.M.T. Children of Hope Foundation Infant Burial, Inc."

An original purpose of the foundation was to provide a dignified funeral and burial for abandoned infants found dead. When adopted by the foundation, each child receives a unique first name, but all share the same surname: Hope. To help with the costs of preparing and transporting the tiny bodies to the funeral Mass and burials, Charles O'Shea, owner of a local funeral home, provides his services at a great discount. Volunteers from the police department perform the ceremony usually reserved for funerals of their deceased comrades. Then each baby is laid to rest at the Holy Rood Cemetery in one of the 16 plots the foundation has purchased. Turnout at the funerals varies in number, ranging from a handful of mourners to more than a hundred local citizens, all wishing to remember in death one who was forgotten during life.[15]

Although one of the central purposes for the A.M.T. Children of Hope is to honor the memory of abandoned infants found dead, the organization's larger goal is preventing such tragedies in the first place. As part of its work, the foundation seeks to prevent infant abandonment by making services available for women in crisis pregnancies and educating the public about the problem of discarded infants. For distressed women, the foundation sponsors a hotline and helps operate a shelter where pregnant mothers can seek counseling and avoid isolation. In addition, the A.M.T. volunteers have lobbied for a safe-havens law, modeled after the ones in Texas and Alabama, so that distressed women can legally relinquish their children without leaving them to die.[16] To increase public awareness about alternatives to abandonment, the foundation publishes educational pamphlets and displays posters at clinics, counseling centers, and train stations throughout New York City and Long Island.[17] Members of the organization have also appeared on the talk shows of hosts such as Montel Williams, Rosie O'Donnell, and Ricki Lake in an effort to educate viewers about the problem of infant abandonment.[18]

The efforts of the A.M.T. Children of Hope Foundation have been successful on multiple levels. They achieved their lobbying goals in July 2000, when New York Governor George Pataki signed into law a statewide safe-havens program. The provisions of this law give a mother affirmative defense to prosecution if she abandons her child of five days or younger at an appropriate location or with a suitable person.[19] After the passage of this legislation, the foundation focused much of its public awareness campaign on helping to make the new law known to those who might consider discarding their infants.

It is difficult to assess the foundation's success in preventing unsafe abandonment because their area of activity has expanded over time from Nassau County to include the entire New York City metropolis. The number of infants they have buried has increased steadily over the years, which may indicate an increase in the number of newborns left to die or perhaps a growing awareness of A.M.T. in the nation's largest city. Lacking statewide or citywide statistics on neonaticide, it is impossible to conclude definitively whether the public awareness endeavors of the A.M.T. Children of Hope Foundation have decreased the instances of infant abandonment. Reports about direct contacts with women in crisis do provide one measure of the foundation's success. Through its help line, the foundation typically receives more than 3,000 calls per year. In 1999, Jaccard, who often answers the calls himself, reported confidently that of "[one hundred] calls to the line, at least [seven] women intent on abandoning their babies chose to give them up for adoption or made arrangements to keep them."[20] If these numbers represent a consistent pattern, the foundation's help line is likely involved in saving more than 200 infants over the course of a year.

Despite the difficulties in quantifying the success of such a program, the compassion and devotion of Jaccard and his willing A.M.T. coworkers have positively influenced the lives of many in Nassau County and the boroughs of New York. Even as the associates of the A.M.T. Children of Hope Foundation continue to perform the tragic rites of death for unclaimed children, those who live to witness these acts of dignity are inspired to value life even more as a result. One man's refusal to ignore the death of a child has enabled his community to appreciate their blessings even more and to find hope in the midst of despair.

THE PROMISE AND PERILS OF GRASSROOTS ACTIVISM

As the previously mentioned profiles of activists and organizations reveal, individuals can and do make a difference when they seek to meet community needs. In each of these cases, a firsthand encounter with the tragedy of infant abandonment touched someone so deeply that he or she responded with direct action. A person or small group of people created a program that began to meet real needs in a community while also capturing local, statewide, and even national attention. Grassroots activism can indeed be a powerful impetus for policy change. Effectiveness at the local level, however, does not necessarily translate into effective nationwide policy. When learning about an issue and developing a network of local level activists, members of Congress and their staff must weigh the extent to which they can learn from and work with grassroots organizations to achieve shared goals. For legislators, working with local groups has benefits but also drawbacks.

LEARNING FROM LOCALS: THE BENEFITS

Having devoted numerous hours of their time and often much of their own money, activists are committed believers in a cause. Founders of organizations are typically the most energized, for they are the ones who were so moved by a situation, problem, or political issue that they created and implemented a plan or group to take action. Many such activists approach their work as a crowning achievement that gives them great purpose and meaning in life. A seemingly simple query posed to the founder of an organization concerning the group's history, purpose, and activities may begin a conversation that could easily stretch for hours. What an outside observer might see as a potentially interesting grassroots effort the founder likely views as a movement of profound personal and political importance. Some activists may become so engrossed in their work that their identity as individuals becomes entwined with the efforts of the cause or organization. To praise the organization is to praise its leader; critiques of the group's work may be construed as personal attacks.

Because of their intense dedication, grassroots activists bring energy and excitement to policy discussions that can be infectious. Activists are true believers; they care deeply about issues and want to convert others to their way of thinking. Many of the most successful grassroots organizers succeed in large part because of their personal charisma. Persuasive and engaging, such leaders will find great success at convincing others of the merits of their cause and boosting morale for ongoing and often tiresome work.

In addition to their dedication and energy, local activists provide a depth of knowledge and understanding of their policy issue that is likely unparalleled. A congressional staffer handles dozens, if not hundreds, of policy issues in a given legislative session. The founder of a single-issue organization, in contrast, can devote his or her full energy to understanding one subject and becoming an expert. On the ground, dealing with a policy issue on a daily basis, grassroots leaders gain practical knowledge of the complexities of their issue. They know what has worked and what has failed in their community because they have seen the results firsthand. Activists also educate themselves. By attending conferences, conducting research, and networking with others who share an interest in similar policies, grassroots leaders develop significant policy expertise.

Local activists played a crucial role in the development of the Safe Havens Support Act. Representative Hart first learned about the concept of safe havens from Patti Weaver, a Pittsburgh mother and activist who founded an organization called "A Hand to Hold." Weaver wrote Melissa Hart, then a state senator, to inform her about the issue and to encourage the creation and passage of a statewide abandoned-infants law. Several years before Pennsylvania passed safe-havens legislation, Weaver's organization had created an informal network to provide assistance to mothers in crisis in the Pittsburgh area. "A Hand to Hold" staffed a twenty four-hour emergency hotline to help women in crisis situations and direct them to a network of hospitals where they could safely relinquish an infant. The Allegheny County District Attorney, in turn, agreed not to prosecute mothers who followed the procedures for safely abandoning infants.[21]

In the early stages of developing the federal legislation, Hart's office contacted Weaver to hear more about her work and learn from her experiences as a local activist. In a series of phone calls and during a meeting in her Pittsburgh-area home, Weaver provided a wealth of information. In addition to giving us several years' worth of news clippings on abandoned infants from a variety of media outlets, she provided contact information for other grassroots activists and offered suggestions for safe-havens legislation. At Hart's invitation, Weaver testified before the Select Education Subcommittee of the House Education and Workforce Committee to discuss her attempts to prevent infant abandonment and to build support for the inclusion of portions of Hart's legislation in the Child Abuse Prevention and Treatment Act.

Hart's office also worked closely with leaders of the "Save Abandoned Babies Foundation," an organization originally based in Northbrook, Illinois. The organization's founder and president, Dawn Geras, first learned about the abandoned-infant issue from a newspaper article about a baby discarded in a dumpster in Chicago.[22] As she began to read more about the problem, Geras learned of Jodi Brooks's work in Alabama and the successful passage of Alabama's safe-havens law. As she explained, "I started to cry. Oh, my God— there are babies being thrown away down in Alabama—Podunk, Alabama— they're doing something about it. In Illinois, we're not. Are we such idiots here?"[23] Spurred to action, Geras shared her vision with friends she knew through her volunteer work with the Make-a-Wish Foundation. Soon she had assembled a group of activists to lobby for a safe-havens bill in Illinois. Their work proved successful: Representative Elizabeth Coulson agreed to sponsor a bill, and the resulting Abandoned Newborn Infant Protection Act went into effect on August 17, 2001. Since then, the definition of "safe havens" has been expanded by Senate Bill 2583 to include police stations, and as of March 31, 2005, fourteen newborns have been safely relinquished to the proper authorities.

WORKING WITH ACTIVISTS: POTENTIAL DRAWBACKS

Local activists bring an impressive combination of knowledge, energy, and devotion to their discussions with policymakers, and legislators will benefit greatly from their interactions with grassroots leaders. But such cooperation is not without its costs.

Many local activists are so engrossed in the particularities of their location and context that they have difficulty seeing the bigger policy picture. Unique circumstances or situations may allow a program that would fail in many areas to flourish in one place. Indeed, what works well in urban areas may not translate as well into more sparsely populated rural counties. In addition, the character, personality, and profession of key activists might play a significant role in a program's success or failure. Would the Mobile program have been as successful, for example, if its champion were not a likable television reporter working for a supportive station? When policymakers seek to replicate programs or borrow ideas, they must consider how a proposal would work in a broader context. Many grassroots activists understand the complexity of exporting policy innovations, but some do not. Legislators and their staff must therefore find a way to acknowledge and commend the contributions of local activists while also considering the bigger picture and creating policies that will be suitable in a larger political context.

In some circumstances, legislators may find that local activists oppose new legislation because the proposed policy would affect the way they operate. Grassroots groups often achieve their goals through informal networks and with little oversight. Although government programs can provide much-needed resources, with government dollars come new regulations and procedures. Local activists may resent what they see as government intrusion on their work. After all, if they have managed to survive and prosper thus far under an existing model, why would they want outsiders telling them how to run their operations? Knowing that change often meets resistance, legislators and their staff may need to approach local activists with a degree of caution when presenting new proposals that might affect ongoing grassroots work.

Furthermore, work with grassroots organizations may reveal long-standing turf battles between groups who use different means to achieve similar policy goals. Each organization has its own style and way of doing its work, with each leader typically believing that his or her approach is the best. Thus, when working with multiple local activists, a congressional office can quickly find itself in the middle of a turf war, with constituents from different groups claiming that their methods in particular should be implemented into law.

Clearly, grassroots activists are an important resource for policymakers seeking to understand more about an issue. Local leaders and organizations provide depth of knowledge and can help forge excellent connections between lawmakers and their constituents, but work with such organizations does have some drawbacks.

CHAPTER SUMMARY

Although scholars note the rise of professional interest-group lobbying in Washington, grassroots organizations still have an important place in American politics. Local activists can and do make an important contribution to addressing public policy issues.

Profiling two organizations at the vanguard of the safe-havens movement, this chapter provided specific examples of concerned individuals who initiated change. After television journalist Jodi Brooks covered several stories about murdered newborns and abandoned infants found dead, she created a network of support with prosecutors and hospitals in Mobile, Alabama, to develop "A Secret Safe Place for Newborns," likely the very first program of its kind in the United States. Paramedic Tim Jaccard began his crusade with a program to provide dignified burials for unclaimed dead babies, founding the organization A.M.T. Children of Hope Foundation Infant Burial, Inc. Through lobbying efforts, public information campaigns, and the provision of direct services, A.M.T. Children of Hope addresses the abandoned-infants issue across Long Island and New York City.

After considering the work of these two organizations, this chapter explained the benefits that grassroots organizations can provide legislators who are working on new policy issues. Local activists have practical knowledge of their policy issue and access to an extensive network of concerned citizens. Energized and committed, grassroots leaders are devoted to their causes. However, working with local activists is not without its drawbacks. Local organizations may not see or understand concerns that affect national policy-making, and groups may have vested interests that create resistance to change.

NOTES

1. "Grassroots," in *The American Heritage Dictionary of the English Language*, 4th ed. (Boston: Houghton Mifflin, 2000).
2. Jo Anne Schneider, "What Is a Grassroots Organization?" Nonprofits.org, September 18, 2003 (accessed at http://www.nonprofits.org/npofaq/18/51.html).
3. Theda Skocpol, "Associations without Members," *The American Prospect* 10 no. 45 (July–August 1999): 66–73.
4. Ibid. Skocpol refers to the increasing numbers of Americans who are "turned off by and pulling back from public life."
5. Ken Kollman, *Outside Lobbying: Public Opinion and Interest Group Strategies* (Princeton, N.J.: Princeton University Press, 1998), 9.
6. Garry Mitchell, "Mobile's Safe Newborns Campaign Catching On," Associated Press, January 8, 2000.
7. Karin Miller, "12-Year-Old Who Was Abandoned Newborn Asks Lawmakers to Approve Safe Haven Law," Associated Press, April 9, 2001.
8. Ibid.
9. Ibid.
10. Jodi Brooks, "Abandoned at Birth: T.V. Reporter Jodi Brooks Talks about a Secret Safe Place for Newborns," CourtTV.com transcript, October 25, 2000 (accessed at http://www.courttv.com/talk/chat_transcripts?102500brooks.html).
11. Miller.
12. Kara Blond, "Guardian of Angels: Paramedic Offers Dignity to Tiny Lives That Had None," *Newsday*, December 30, 1998 (accessed at http://www.amtchildrenofhope.com/press1.htm/).
13. Randal C. Archibold, "Dignity for the Tiniest Victims: Paramedics Arrange Funerals for Abandoned Infants," *The New York Times*, December 7, 1999 (accessed at http://www.amtchildrenofhope.com/press5.htm/).
14. Ibid.
15. Jacqueline L. Salmon, "For Unwanted Babies, a Safety Net: More States Offer 'Havens' to Deter Abandonment, but Critics Abound," *Washington Post*, January 1, 2004.
16. Archibold.

17. "Who We Are," A.M.T. Children of Hope Foundation (accessed at http://www.amtchildrenofhope.com/profile.htm).
18. "Safe Haven Laws," A.M.T. Children of Hope Foundation (accessed at http://smtchildrenofhope.com/safe_haven_law.htm).
19. Archibold.
20. "About Us," Save Abandoned Babies Foundation (accessed at http://www.saveabandonedbabies.org/about.shtml).
21. "Will There Be a Hand to Hold?" A Hand to Hold (accessed at http://www.ahandtohold.org/).
22. "Timeline," Save Abandoned Babies Foundation (accessed at http://www.saveabandonedbabies.org/about.shtml).
23. Irv Leavitt, "Two Try to Spotlight Their 2001 Abandoned Baby Law," *Northbrook Star*, December 26, 2002 (accessed at http://archives.pioneerlocal.com/cgi-bin/ppo-story/archives/localnews/2002/nb/12-12-02-54320.html).

THE SEARCH FOR SOLUTIONS

Transferring Ideas into Policy

Conducting background research and building connections with interest groups and grassroots organizations are important initial steps toward the goal of creating public policy. For Representative Hart's office, after completing most of the background work on safe havens, the next priority was translating abstract ideas and concepts about safe havens into a concrete bill. To accomplish this goal, the staff needed to evaluate existing state safe-havens laws to look for ways that a new federal law could complement the work already in progress in these states. With this information, the congresswoman could decide what legislation to propose and could begin drafting the final language of the bill.

Following Hart's office through these next crucial stages of policy development, this chapter describes the benefits and tensions of federalism—the division of powers between state and national governments—and traces the process of evaluating current state action to determine what the federal government could and should do to address the problem of infant abandonment. It also describes the components of a typical bill and introduces the Office of Legislative Counsel, a team of attorneys who help lawmakers transform policy ideas into legislative language.

Leading the Way: States as Sources of Innovation

Federalism, the system of sovereign powers shared between a national government and state governments, gives states the freedom to be different from one another. Since each state creates its own governing structure and writes its own laws, states can directly address the problems affecting their residents and can be more responsive to specific needs. Thus, for example, states along the border with Mexico will likely implement more policies that address immigration than those less affected by waves of Mexican immigrants. Coastal states with major ports of entry for international trade will be more concerned with safety regulations for imported cargo than landlocked states such as South Dakota and Kansas. As individual states confront emerging issues, their governments will attempt to address their specific problems, sometimes with policy solutions that have never before been attempted.

Because the governments of the fifty states can design and implement new policy ideas, states are an important source of innovation. Congress can look to the various states to see what, if anything, they have accomplished on a given issue, thus finding new ideas for federal solutions. In addition, many members of Congress served in state legislatures before winning federal office, so they often bring ideas with them from their previous experiences.

Like most of her colleagues with state legislative experience, Melissa Hart brought to Washington a legislative agenda built from her time in the Pennsylvania senate. Hart was well versed in the work that states had been doing to create infant safe havens, especially since she had already introduced her own bill as a Pennsylvania senator. Congress had yet to pass significant legislation on this issue, but state governments were moving ahead at a rapid pace, passing and implementing new laws designed to create safe havens that would discourage a parent from abandoning a baby in an unsafe place. Successes and failures at the state level would inform decisions made when writing a federal bill.

The flood of safe-havens legislation began in 1999 with the unanimous passage of Texas H.B. 3423. Shocked by reports of a string of infant abandonments around Houston (five discarded babies were found in a period of two weeks), legislators and activists in Texas began to act on the problem. Fort Worth doctor John Richardson provided the initial momentum for legislation. After reading about women in crisis, Richardson approached his niece who, in turn, presented his idea of **infant safe havens** to Texas state representative Geanie Morrison. Morrison, a member of the Juvenile Justice and Family Issues Committee, wrote H.B. 3423. According to the provisions of what Morrison calls the "Baby Moses" bill, a parent who brings a healthy infant less than thirty days old to any place licensed to provide emergency medical services will be given an affirmative defense, a legal rationale that prosecutors could use to dismiss criminal action against the parent. The bill received broad-based support, passing unanimously in both chambers of the Texas legislature. On June 6, 1999, then-Governor George W. Bush signed the nation's first infant safe-havens bill into law. In the next legislative session, Representative Morrison introduced related legislation, H.B. 706, that refined the initial safe-havens statute. The provisions of this new law grant immunity to parents who safely relinquish a child, increase the age limit for an eligible infant from thirty to sixty days, and expand safe havens to include all hospitals and qualified child placement facilities.

Aware that legislation alone was only a first step in combating the problem of infant abandonment, Morrison and Dr. Richardson created the "Baby Moses

Project" to increase education and awareness about the availability of infant safe havens in Texas. Organizers explain the purpose of the project and its connection to the biblical story of the infant Moses:

> In addition to being placed in a basket, Moses was also carefully watched over by an anonymous protector until he was safely placed in the arms of a person who could provide the love and care necessary for life. Similarly, those involved with this project and the implementation of abandonment legislation want to provide a protector for newborns and anonymity for desperate mothers who choose a responsible alternative to abandonment.[1]

Project organizers created public service announcements, designed a Web site, and began outreach efforts to encourage the creation and awareness of infant safe-havens programs in other states.

LABORATORIES OF DEMOCRACY: LEARNING FROM THE STATES

Just as state governments introduce and implement new political solutions, so states serve as a resource for testing the effectiveness of different ways to achieve similar policy goals. Former Supreme Court Justice Louis Brandeis used the metaphor "laboratories of democracy" to describe this phenomenon.[2] When states implement new laws that are similar but contain varying guidelines and directives, each state becomes a testing ground for measuring the effectiveness of its particular law. Congress can compare the impact of various provisions and also assess the potential benefits and drawbacks of each. If new programs in one state lead to demonstrated improvements, Congress may want to use the policy as a template for national legislation. Conversely, if state experiments reveal unanticipated problems in the implementation of a new law, Congress can learn from these mistakes and then design corrective measures.[3]

The idea of state experimentation is not, however, a license for any and all types of innovation. There are at least two conditions that must be met for the laboratory concept to work: Experimentation must be limited to citizens within a state's borders, and there must be limitations on national power so that the federal government cannot force experiments on unwilling states. For a recent example that illustrates the need for these principles, consider the deregulation of electricity. By most accounts, the programs in Texas, Pennsylvania, and Virginia have been successful. Conversely, the attempt at deregulation in California was a dismal failure, leading to a series of blackouts and contributing to the recall and replacement of then-Governor Gray Davis. Other states can learn from the profitable policies of the successful states, borrowing specific policy ideas and legislative language from them.

Even problematic state experiments have policy value, as they help legislators avoid the mistakes of the failed programs and learn important lessons for planning future attempts at reform.

Another recent example of federalism in the national spotlight is the debate over the legality of same-sex marriages. The lack of consensus on the constitutionality of homosexual marriage has placed this divisive issue firmly in the jurisdiction of the states. Both gay rights activists and conservative lobbying groups have been endeavoring to promote their beliefs at the state level. In May 2004, for example, the state of Massachusetts legalized gay marriage, joining Vermont, a state that currently recognizes civil unions. While some states moved toward recognizing such unions, others implemented policy designed to prevent it. In August 2004, Missouri passed a constitutional ban on gay marriage; Louisiana followed suit in September, and eleven other states passed election-day referenda against same-sex marriage that November.

Surprisingly, people on both sides of the issue believe that the results of such state experimentation will lead to national gains for them in the long run. Proponents of gay rights raise this argument: "Eventually, the people of some state will cross the line and recognize gay marriage formally. And when that does not cause the sky to fall, the decision will be emulated in other states."[4] Conversely, opponents of gay marriage expect that state experimentation will have the opposite effect: "These state amendments are a political dress rehearsal for the federal marriage amendment."[5] On both sides of the same-sex marriage issue, the warring parties have found one point of unanimous agreement: Public policy decisions made in the states will have profound policy implications for the rest of the country.

Laboratories of democracy seem especially important in the current political climate. Historically, political liberals have advocated for federal government solutions to policy problems. In the battle for civil rights, for example, movement activists found federal court rulings and congressional action to be essential tools for overcoming discriminatory state laws. In more recent political debates, however, activists from the left have rediscovered "the states' role in the federal system as 'laboratories of democracy.' In many areas of public policy, state legislators have become the vanguard of the progressive movement."[6] Many conservative activists have adopted a similar view of the role of the states in policy development: "Successful state and local experiments with airline deregulation, welfare reform, and school choice taught valuable lessons, built confidence in innovative policies, and provided a testing ground for social scientists' models and policy recommendations that might well have gone unheeded in a centralized political environment."[7] Conservatives and liberals alike seem to agree that success in the current public policy context often begins with the states.

SAFE HAVENS IN THE STATES

Hart's office understood the importance of looking to the states for policy innovation. By the time we began working on a federal safe-havens law, thirty states had already passed some form of safe-havens statute, and several others were considering similar proposals. With laws in effect in so many states, Hart could look at examples from across the country for ideas about how to shape a federal law.

The specific content of safe-havens bills varies from state to state, but all serve a common purpose: Saving lives by diminishing or removing the threat of criminal prosecution against parents who relinquish unharmed infants to identified safe havens. Existing laws have many specific provisions in common. They all designate locations or people to whom a parent in crisis can surrender a newborn, and they all provide some form of relief to a parent who chooses to safely relinquish an infant. In about half the states, a parent receives immunity from criminal prosecution; in the others, the decision to relinquish a baby safely guarantees an affirmative defense to prosecution. Most statutes protect the anonymity of the parent, while others require workers at a safe haven to encourage the parent to provide a basic family medical history. Under most versions of the law, those who accept a relinquished infant are free from liability; state child welfare officials take custody of the baby and arrange for foster care and eventual adoption. In addition, many of the provisions allow the parent a period of time in which to reconsider relinquishing a baby. Typically, if a parent brings a newborn to a safe haven and then changes his or her mind, the parent can, after undergoing counseling, reunite with the infant. The age of infants eligible for safe-havens programs in each state varies from seventy-two hours old to a year old, with most laws applicable for babies either seventy-two hours old and younger or thirty days old and younger.

While a few states had speedily passed safe-havens laws, most of the laws were still new at the time I began researching the issue. No one had yet collected and analyzed data in any systematic way, but early reports from the states suggested that safe-havens laws did not lead to dramatic increases in instances of infant abandonment. Preliminary findings seemed to indicate that, in the states and areas that conducted campaigns to inform the public about these laws, the number of infants abandoned and left to die had declined. Some mothers had indeed relinquished their newborns under the protection of the new statutes.

Because representatives knew it would be more difficult to build support for a bill that requires state spending, sponsors in most states wrote legislation that simply changed the criminal code. As a result, very few state safe-havens laws include any funding to inform the public about the new policy. Anecdotal evidence from the states suggests that news about safe havens is not easily reaching the people in greatest need: Pregnant women who have made no preparation for parenting. Although some parents do know about safe havens and have chosen to safely relinquish newborns, unlawful abandonment continues in states with these laws in place and is most common in states without public information campaigns. Despite the wave of publicity when Geanie Morrison's bill passed in Texas, for instance, several parents abandoned infants unsafely instead of taking their infants to a safe haven. Now that the Baby Moses Project and other Texas organizations have begun to advertise the availability of safe-havens options, several infants have been safely relinquished.

FINDING THE FEDERAL ISSUES: A ROLE FOR CONGRESS?

Unlike a unitary system of government with one central, sovereign government that holds authority over states, the federal design created in the U.S. Constitution divides power between the states and the national government, giving states some independent authority. Article I of the Constitution delegates exclusive powers to Congress for seventeen types of activity, such as coining money, regulating interstate commerce, and declaring war. The states, in turn, are given a few enumerated powers, including conducting elections, appointing members of the electoral college to select the president, and addressing concerns of public health, safety, and morals. Several important powers, including taxation, establishing courts, and making and enforcing laws, are granted to both the state and national governments. In those instances when state and federal laws conflict, the Constitution explicitly grants supremacy to the national government, but the Tenth Amendment grants states control over all areas of jurisdiction not explicitly delineated in the Constitution.

Over the course of American history, the boundaries between the state and national government have changed. Whereas the federal government had a relatively limited role for more than a century, the scope and bounds of federal law expanded greatly in the twentieth century. A dramatic shift occurred during the presidency of Franklin Roosevelt, whose New Deal programs extended federal government control to include a wide array of social policies, such as social security and poor support, that had previously been left to the states. The power and scope of federal government continued to expand for decades thereafter.

Concerns about Washington taking too much control led to a new era of federalism that began with the presidency of Ronald Reagan and continues to the present day. Under the principles of **devolution,** government leaders (primarily within the Republican Party) have implemented many policies designed to return more power to the states. The Rehnquist court contributed to the process as well, ruling in a series of cases regarding federalism that the federal government overstepped its bounds, encroaching on powers that should be left to the states.

Aware of the judicial climate on issues of federalism, many members of Congress try to anticipate Supreme Court action when crafting laws. Some legislators will introduce legislation they know will face a strong challenge in the courts, but pragmatic members introduce bills that they believe will survive constitutional scrutiny. So, when designing a new bill, legislators ask the question, Which actions are within the powers of Congress, and which ones appear to be outside its constitutional authority?

When writing what would become the Safe Havens Support Act, the research led me to a simple but stark conclusion: The government structure and division of authority make it very difficult, if not impossible, to create a federal safe-havens statute. First, such a bill would raise constitutional issues. In an era of power devolving to the states, the Supreme Court is less likely to uphold federal laws that expand the powers expressly given to Congress. Since a federal law creating safe havens might amend or nullify existing state criminal statutes, such a law would likely be overturned. Second, even if found to be constitutional, a federal safe-havens statute would be a logistical nightmare. Each state has its own criminal statutes that categorize crimes and assign penalties, its own child welfare system, its own set of laws governing paternity, and its own procedures for adoption. A federal law navigating so many areas of jurisdiction would be, at best, incredibly complex and, at worst, almost impossible to administer.

After conducting enough background research to begin designing a new policy, I wrote a memo to the congresswoman detailing various items she might choose to include in a federal safe-havens bill. The memo first summarized the related laws already in place at the state level and then outlined several ways the federal government could help the states. These included commissioning a national study of the problem of infant abandonment and giving states funds to help inform the public about safe-havens laws. Unable to decide on a specific amount needed to pay for these programs, we left the dollar figure blank pending further research and discussion.

The congresswoman met with senior staff to discuss the memo and give direction about how to write her bill. Although she was disappointed that the creation of a federal safe-havens statute was unrealistic, she liked the goals listed in the memo and agreed that the federal government needed to help states educate the public about safe havens and needed to collect better data. A fiscal conservative, she balked at the idea of adding money to the federal budget and noted that some Republicans would not support any spending bill regardless of subject matter. Hart argued that the Department of Health and Human Services could conduct the national study as part of its general operations budget. We discussed ways to pay for the education parts of the proposal with existing money but could not find a satisfactory solution. After much discussion, Hart reluctantly agreed that the bill should include a spending clause. Existing state programs lacked money to pay for public information campaigns and technical assistance; this bill could provide the much-needed funds, and new federal spending seemed the only option. The basic template prepared, it was time to turn these ideas into policy.

HOW OLD IS AN INFANT? DRAFTING H.R. 2018

Once the congresswoman and her senior staff agreed on its basic components, it was time to write a first draft of the bill. Although many details had yet to be decided, we concurred in the following:

- The name of the bill should be "Safe Havens Support Act."
- The bill should include a definitions section that would allow states freedom to establish and define safe havens as they choose while at the same time moving them toward more uniform definitions of key terms.
- The Department of Health and Human Services should conduct a study to determine the number of infants abandoned (including how many such infants died) and the number of infants murdered each year and should also study the characteristics of women at risk of abandoning their newborns.

WRITING AN INITIAL DRAFT

With these provisions in mind, I wrote a draft bill. Typically, a bill begins with a short sentence or two defining the purpose of the legislation followed by a short title chosen by the bill's sponsor. Hence, the draft began, "To establish a program that would assist states and organizations to implement programs that facilitate the safe relinquishment of newborn infants," and went on to identify the legislation as the "Safe Havens Support Act of 2001."

FINDINGS

Many bills include "findings," a section beginning with the phrase "Congress finds that . . . ," followed by a series of declaratory statements that the sponsor wants written directly into the law. Some bills include statistical data in this section; others include opinion statements designed to make a political point. Often legislators use this section of a bill to include facts and arguments supporting their cause. In the Partial-Birth Abortion Ban Act of 2003, for example, opponents of the procedure wrote eleven paragraphs of findings that specifically addressed a previous Supreme Court ruling and argued why the law as written should survive any constitutional challenges.

Hart's office was uncertain about the need for a findings section in the Safe Havens Support Act. If used to make political points, findings can add to the controversy over a bill. In this case, the goal was to build a bipartisan coalition of support, so we wanted to avoid anything that would impede that goal. In addition, we had little reliable data about the prevalence of infant abandonment in the United States. Thus, in the end, Hart decided not to include findings.

DESIGNING A POLICY PROGRAM

The middle sections of a bill set forth the new or revised policy and provide direction for its implementation. Bills creating complex policy programs may include hundreds of pages of specific provisions describing the use and purpose of federal funds.

Congress usually distributes money to states and organizations through one of two types of federal grants: **block grants** or **categorical grants**. Block grants offer states flexibility, giving money in large "blocks" with a broad set of guidelines that give states flexibility in how specifically to spend the funds. Categorical grants, in contrast, offer federal money to recipients with more specific instructions for how the money must be used. These grants often require **matching funds**; that is, the government or organization receiving the federal grant must contribute some of its own funding to help pay for the project or service. Legislation creating a grant program will also include language stating who is eligible to receive grants and detailing the process for distributing the funds. One type of grant, a **formula grant**, disperses money using some kind of arithmetic calculation. A program to assist families in poverty, for example, may allocate money on the basis of the percentage of state residents living below the poverty line. Another option, a **competitive grant**, requires recipients to compete for funding. Government agencies or organizations that hope to receive funds submit applications demonstrating how they would use the money and why they are well suited to provide the expected service.

In the process of deciding which type of grant program to include in Hart's bill, I consulted an expert from the Congressional Research Service (CRS) who faxed samples of legislative language creating different types of federal grant programs. After comparing the options, we decided to design a competitive grant process that would allow both government agencies and nonprofit organizations in states with safe-havens programs to apply for funding. The examples faxed from the CRS served as templates for the draft language.

The original draft of a simple bill like the Safe Havens Support Act included only two short policy sections. Patterned after Public Law 100-505, the Abandoned Infants Assistance Act that dealt with drug-addicted and HIV-infected babies left in hospitals, section 3 established a grant program so that states with safe havens in place could apply for funding to help with public information campaigns and technical assistance. This section established parameters for the kinds of projects allowed, detailed the requirements for grant applications, and permitted the Department of Health and Human Services to train and assist organizations trying to implement safe-havens projects.

Reflecting our office's concern that little accurate data existed to measure the scope of the problem, the next section commissioned an annual study to estimate and report the number of infants abandoned, relinquished, and found dead each year as well as to identify characteristics of parents at risk of abandoning their babies.

DEFINING TERMS

Most bills that create new policies include a **definitions section** at the beginning or end that clarifies potentially ambiguous terms. Our original draft of the Safe Havens Support Act defined five such terms: Abandoned infant, designated safe haven, relinquish, eligible nonprofit entities, and secretary. The bill defined "abandoned infant" for two specific reasons. First, the age of infants defined in state safe-havens legislation varied significantly, from less than seventy-two hours old to under a year old. We wanted to include as many state programs as possible but at the same time focus attention on the crisis surrounding relatively newborn infants; thus, we chose to include infants thirty days old or less. In addition, the bill explained the meaning of "abandoned" as it applied to this legislation. Given the confusion between babies left in hospitals covered under the Abandoned Infants Assistance Act and those infants discarded and left to die, the definition clarified the term to include infants "intentionally left or discarded by a parent unwilling or unable to care for the infant."

"Designated safe haven" was another important definition. Aware that some states (including Hart's own, Pennsylvania) did not have safe-havens laws but did have programs in place that would provide a parent in crisis a safe option for abandoning a baby without fear of prosecution, we defined the term to incorporate all such programs that served the same goal.

AUTHORIZING FUNDING

Finally, all legislation that calls for federal spending must include a section for **authorization of appropriations**. Congress makes budget decisions in a two-step process. Bills that create federal programs "authorize" spending; that is, they give the government the authority to spend stated sums of money for a given purpose. In order to distribute the funds authorized by legislation, however, Congress must pass annual **appropriations bills** that detail the actual amount of money given to each authorized program. Congress authorizes far more spending than it actually approves, so there is no guarantee that a program passed into law will receive its complete (or even partial) funding in the appropriations process. In fact, some programs that are technically created never actually exist because Congress does not approve funding for them.

FIGURE 5.1: THE FIRST DRAFT OF THE ORIGINAL SAFE HAVENS SUPPORT ACT

A Bill

To establish a program that would assist states and organizations to implement programs that facilitate the safe relinquishment of newborn infants.

SECTION 1: SHORT TITLE

This Act may be cited as the "Safe Havens Support Act of 2001"

SECTION 2: FINDINGS

The Congress finds that—

SECTION 3: GRANTS FOR THE PROMOTION AND ASSISTANCE OF SAFE HAVEN PROJECTS

Title I: Public Information Campaigns

(a) In General—The Secretary of Health and Human Services (the Secretary), in consultation with the Attorney General, may make grants to public and eligible nonprofit private entities for the purpose of developing, implementing, and operating projects that:
  (1) inform them about existing means for relinquishing a newborn to designated safe havens as outlined in state laws or agreements between local prosecutors and healthcare providers
  (2) educate children and/or adults about legal infant relinquishment options
  (3) provide a designated toll-free information line to direct individuals to locations authorized to accept relinquished or abandoned infants and provide information about infant relinquishment laws or agreements
  (4) train and educate health care workers, public safety officers or any other individuals authorized to accept abandoned or relinquished infants to familiarize them with the designated safe haven procedures for accepting such an infant and caring for the parent relinquishing the infant
  (5) recruit and train health and social services personnel to work with relinquished or abandoned infants, their families and prospective adoptive families
(b) Requirements of Application—The Secretary may not make a grant under subsection (a) unless—
  (1) an application for the grant is submitted to the secretary;
  (2) with respect to carrying out the purpose for which the grant is to be made, the application provides assurances of compliance satisfactory to the Secretary; and

---

continued

(3) the application otherwise is in such form, is made in such manner, and contains such agreements, assurances, and information as the Secretary determines is necessary to carry out this section.

(4) The Secretary will give preference to collaborative efforts between more than one eligible public or private agency

(c) Technical Assistance to Grantees—The Secretary may, without charge to any grantee under subsection (a), provide technical assistance (including training) with respect to the planning, development, and operation of such projects described in such subsection. The Secretary may provide such technical assistance directly, through contracts, or through grants.

(d) Technical Assistance with Respect to Process of Applying for Grant—The Secretary may provide technical assistance (including training) to public and nonprofit entities with respect to the process of applying for a grant under subsection (a). The Secretary may provide such technical assistance directly, through contracts, or through grants.

SECTION 4: EVALUATIONS, STUDIES, AND REPORTS BY SECRETARY

(a) Evaluation of Demonstration Projects—The Secretary shall, directly or through contracts with public and nonprofit private entities, provide for evaluations of projects carried out under section 3 and for the dissemination of information developed as a result of such projects.

(b) Study and Report on Number of Abandoned Infants
(1) The Secretary shall conduct a study for the purpose for determining—
(A) an estimate of the number of infants abandoned and relinquished within thirty days of birth;
(B) an estimate of the number of infants who are found dead and the number who survive
(C) characteristics and demographics of parents at risk to abandon newborn infants
(2) The Secretary shall, not later than 12 months after the date of the enactment of this Act, complete the study required in paragraph (1) and submit to the Congress a report describing the findings made as a result of this study

SECTION 5: DEFINITIONS

Abandoned Infant—a newborn infant, not more than 30 days old, intentionally left or discarded by a parent unwilling or unable to care for the infant

Designated Safe Haven—state laws or area programs that provide immunity or affirmative defense to parents who relinquish infants in accordance

continued

with a state law or local agreement between local prosecuting authorities and medical facilities

Relinquish—surrendering custody of a newborn infant, not more than 30 days old, under designated safe haven provisions

Eligible Nonprofit Private Entities—[to be provided]

Secretary—the Secretary of Health and Human Services

SECTION 6: AUTHORIZATION OF APPROPRIATIONS

For the purpose of making grants under section 3, there are authorized to be appropriated $00,000,000 for fiscal year 2002 and such sums as necessary.

Source: Office of Congresswoman Melissa A. Hart (PA-04).

Since the safe-havens bill created grant programs, the legislation had to include a final section that authorized federal spending. Although Hart was reluctant to sponsor legislation increasing federal spending, she knew the bill would have to allocate tens of millions of dollars to have any effect. While the congresswoman mulled over the exact figure to include in this section, her staff circulated a bill summary without a definitive annual cost for the program.

INTEREST GROUPS AND LEGISLATIVE LANGUAGE

As they do in other stages during the process of transforming an idea into a bill, outside groups can play an important role in drafting legislation. Some lobbyists might present legislators with drafts of bills that are complete and ready to introduce; others may suggest minor changes to an existing proposal. If an organization has a reputation for providing sound advice and carefully crafting legislative language, congressional staff may directly request its help. Conversely, some lobbyists, on learning that a member is working on a bill, will initiate the contact in order to pressure him or her to modify the language of draft legislation.

As we began writing the Safe Havens Support Act, Hart's staff consulted several outside groups for feedback. One person who provided specific suggestions was Patti Weaver, an activist with a Pittsburgh-area safe-havens program. Drawing from her own research and experiences while founding "A Hand to Hold," Weaver stressed the importance of establishing a designated toll-free information hotline. She noted that information lines in some states route calls to general crisis numbers whose operators may have little knowledge of the applicable laws and available resources. Activists in Texas had even reported to her that callers to an abandoned-infants hotline were routed to an abortion clinic. Thus, she counseled, we should include language to ensure that any toll-free information lines would connect directly to an operator trained specifically to inform parents in crisis of safe-havens options.

Outside groups also assisted in the drafting process by offering constructive criticism of the language we proposed. After we had written an initial draft of the bill, I forwarded it to some of the interest-group staff members who had provided input earlier in the process. Barbara Allen at the Child Welfare League of America (CWLA) responded to the request and suggested several modifications. Representing child welfare professionals in all fifty states, the CWLA was particularly attuned to the disparities between various states' safe-havens programs. Hart's was the first federal law directly addressing safe havens, so the definitions section provided an opportunity to move the states toward uniform standards.

THE OFFICE OF LEGISLATIVE COUNSEL

Legislative language is very precise, technical, and rather arcane, so the typical congressional staffer is poorly equipped to write a bill. Hence, when members of the House are ready to begin drafting legislation, they can contact the House Office of Legislative Counsel (HLC), the sole purpose of which is to "to advise and assist the House of Representatives, and its committees and members, in the achievement of a clear, faithful, and coherent expression of legislative policies."[8] **Legislative counsel** offices in both the House and the Senate provide teams of trained attorneys who can help legislators transform their diverse policy ideas into standard legislative language.

Under present law, the Speaker of the House appoints the legislative counsel, who then, subject to the approval of the Speaker, may choose his or her own assistants. Currently, the HLC employs about thirty-five attorneys and fifteen support staff.[9] Unlike many other government offices, this one office contains no subcommittees or formal departments. Instead, the attorneys cooperate to divide the work as evenly as possible. For the sake of efficiency, individual employees often develop expertise and specialize in a certain area of federal law, or they work in groups on legislation. As lawyers in the office draft legislation, their guiding principle is to give impartial advice about a bill's legal implications. They must maintain the confidentiality demanded by rules of attorney–client privilege, and statute forbids them to "advocate the adoption or rejection of any legislation."[10] Rather, the lawyers combine knowledge about legal limitations with their expertise in legislative drafting to translate a legislator's policy interests into a workable law. Often this involves meeting with members of the House and their staff, attending relevant House committee sessions, and consulting experts in a given field. The final goal is legislation that accurately contains a member's specific policy ideas in good drafting form and style.

The art of transforming a legislator's policy goals into proper legal language is complex and requires much training. As one attorney in the HLC explained, "Drafting legislation is without question a matter of on-the-job training. For up to two years, a new attorney in the Office . . . works under the tutelage of a senior attorney in preparing for introduction a wide variety of bills to gain as much experience as possible in developing drafting skills."[11] Given the highly technical nature of the work and the ready availability of an entire staff of professionals devoted to drafting legislative language, most members, senators, and committees rely on their respective Offices of Legislative Counsel to write bills for them.

When Hart's office contacted the HLC to assist with writing the Safe Havens Support Act, we had an initial draft that included the general points Hart wanted to communicate, some rudimentary definitions, and the policy goals of the bill. We knew that the HLC would sharpen the language and take care of the technical details. In conversation with the attorney assigned to draft the bill, I further explained its goals along with details that Hart thought should be included.

CHANGING HORSES MIDSTREAM

While the legislative counsel began working on his first version of the bill, Hart was circulating the summary of her draft version to build interest in it. As discussed in chapter 3, Congresswoman Hart met with several caucuses to discuss her plan for safe-havens legislation and to enlist her colleagues' support. One such group was the Republican Study Committee (RSC). At a regular members' meeting, Hart circulated the draft proposal that included an authorization for new spending and asked RSC members to cosponsor the bill. After this meeting, the RSC's executive director, Neil Bradley, called the office.

The *National Journal* describes Bradley as a rising star: "At only twenty five, Bradley is among the most powerful staffers in the House." He began working on Capitol Hill when he was a freshman at Georgetown University, starting as an intern in Representative Tom Coburn's office and moving to a full-time paid staff position even as he continued his studies. By the time he graduated from college, he was Coburn's legislative director and had built a reputation as "a leading voice for House conservatives."[12] Bradley moved to his position with the RSC after Coburn retired from the House.

Most of the ninety members of the RSC are fiscal conservatives, and several refuse to support any legislation that adds to federal spending, regardless of the subject matter of the bill. Bradley suggested a way we could change the proposal and not spend any new money, thus increasing the likelihood of gaining a conservative's support.

Specifically, he alerted me to surpluses in the Temporary Assistance to Needy Families (TANF) program. TANF resulted from the comprehensive welfare reform measures that President Clinton signed into law; it gave each state large block grants to support a variety of programs that assist needy families. Almost three years into this new program, many states were not spending the entirety of their federal awards. Whereas eight states had spent all or virtually all of their TANF money, forty-two other states and the District of Columbia had surpluses that ranged from $89,769 in Virginia to almost $1.2 billion in New York. Bradley suggested we fund our bill by amending TANF to allow states the option to use some of their surplus money for safe-havens programs. Instead of authorizing new federal spending, this change would simply give states access to unspent federal money. Such a proposal would appeal to many pro-life conservatives who shared the goal of saving the lives of newborns but, on principle, never supported bills that increased government spending.

Our office would never have discovered the TANF surpluses without the creativity and assistance of Bradley and the RSC. Because Representative Hart discussed the bill with the RSC during the drafting process, she received constructive feedback that helped her build greater support for the bill while at the same time reshaping the draft legislation so it would be more to their liking.

Having found a way to fund safe-havens support programs without increasing federal spending, Hart decided to change the bill. I called the attorney at legislative counsel and told him about the new direction. Assisting safe-havens programs through a federal competitive grant process was out; expanding TANF so that states could use excess funds to create public information campaigns was in. Accustomed to congressional offices calling with multiple changes to legislation in the drafting process, the attorney took the new directions in stride. Amending TANF to add an allowable use of funds was much simpler than creating a new federal program, so he told us to expect a draft bill in a matter of days.

Hart's office received a discussion draft of the new bill on May 9, 2001. Unlike the six-section rendition we gave to the HLC, their new version included just three sections covering four and a half pages. The first section, the short title, remained the same. A new section 2, "TANF funds authorized to be used for infant safe havens programs," amended the welfare bill to allow states the option to use money "to support an infant safe haven program." Additional language here defined terms. Unlike our original draft that included a relatively simple definition of "infant safe haven program," the HLC's definition was an expansive, thirty-eight-line description of the purposes and possible activities of such a program. The new version also added a short definition of the term "support" and described two additional related terms: "newborn baby" and "relinquish." A third and final section directed Health and Human Services to collect data on infant abandonment along the lines outlined in the original draft. Although the wording varied dramatically from the preliminary version I had written, the new one achieved the same policy ends in much more descriptive and technical language.

Generally pleased with the HLC version, Hart suggested only minor changes. We then asked the HLC to prepare a final draft for the congresswoman.

CHAPTER SUMMARY

Members of Congress consider prospective legislation in the context of American federalism, the system of sovereign powers shared between a national government and state governments. The Constitution divides power between the national and state governments, so states have the power to create their own governing structures and to write their own laws. Thus, when replicating a state policy at the federal level, members of Congress must determine what actions the Constitution allows.

By the time that Hart's office began working on a federal safe-havens law, thirty states had already passed some form of safe-havens statute, and several others were considering similar proposals. States write their own criminal codes, raising great difficulties for implementing a federal safe-havens statute. Experience from the states, however, did uncover several ways the federal government could promote and assist safe-havens programs.

With advice from interest-group staff, Hart's office wrote a draft bill that included a definitions section to explain key terms, created a grant program to assist safe-havens programs with public information campaigns, and commissioned a study of the number of infants abandoned each year. A legislative attorney from the House Office of Legislative Counsel, the support office created to help members of Congress draft legislation, sharpened the draft language and wrote a final version of what would soon become the Safe Havens Support Act.

NOTES

1. Baby Moses Project (accessed at http://www.babymosesproject.org).
2. Michael S. Greve, "Laboratories of Democracy: Anatomy of a Metaphor," Federalism-project.org, May 2001 (accessed at http://ww.federalismproject.org/outlook/5-2001.html).
3. For more discussion of the dynamics of federalism, see Martha Derthick, *Keeping the Compound Republic: Essays on American Federalism* (Washington, D.C.: Brookings Institution Press, 2001), and Paul Peterson, Barry G. Rabe, and Kenneth K. Wong, *When Federalism Works* (Washington, D.C.: Brookings Institution Press, 1986).
4. Bruce Ledewitz, "The Bright Future of Gay Marriage," *Pittsburgh Post-Gazette*, November 14, 2004.

5. "Eleven US States Outlaw Gay Marriage in Legislative Sweep," *Agence France Presse*, November 3, 2004.

6. Ralph Nader, "State Legislatures as 'Laboratories of Democracy,'" Commondreams.org, May 31, 2004 (accessed at http://www.commondreams.org/views04/0531-12.htm).

7. Greve.

8. "About HOLC," U.S. House of Representatives Office of the Legislative Counsel, August 13, 2003 (accessed at http://legcoun.house.gov/about.html).

9. 2 USC § 281a.

10. Sandra Strokoff, "How Our Laws Are Made: A Ghost Writer's View," U.S. House of Representatives Office of the Legislative Counsel, August 13, 2003 (accessed at http://legcoun.house.gov/ghost.html).

11. 2 USC § 281a.

12. Lisa Caruso, Keith Heath Koffler, and Erin Wodele, "Key House Groups," *National Journal* 35 no. 25 (June 21, 2003): 1988.

WINNING FRIENDS TO INFLUENCE PEOPLE

Cosponsors and Coalitions

Now that Representative Hart had a solid working draft of the Safe Havens Support Act, she needed to build a bipartisan coalition of supporters. She knew that a clear and concise policy, backed by a large bipartisan group of members and organizations, would demonstrate a base of strong support for assisting safe-havens programs and helping to generate momentum for the issue. The next step in the process, then, was to find a way of bringing together Democrats and Republicans who favored the proposal.

As a freshman Republican elected in a predominantly Democratic district, Hart wanted to avoid narrowly partisan politics and build a reputation as a team player. She sought to build positive working relationships across party lines, so she knew that she needed to identify issues and policies that would appeal to both Republicans and Democrats. She also knew that her ten years in the Pennsylvania senate would provide a basis from which to begin her federal legislative agenda. Looking back at her work in Pennsylvania, she could use past successes to identify issues and legislation that would likely work well in the House of Representatives.

The safe-havens issue was a natural fit. Hart had introduced a safe-havens bill in Pennsylvania and found a solid base of bipartisan support. Although the bill had not yet passed, she was optimistic it would succeed in the near future. From her experience in Pennsylvania, she knew that this was a good issue for most Republicans and Democrats and that, if sold correctly, it would receive wide acceptance from fellow legislators.

This chapter describes patterns of partisanship in the contemporary Congress and methods members use to bridge the partisan divide. After explaining the role of coalitions in building support for legislation, the chapter traces the process of securing Republican and Democratic cosponsors and enlisting help from party leadership to build momentum in favor of a bill.

Finding Common Ground on an Uncommon Issue

Few issues divide legislators as starkly as that of abortion. Most lawmakers are very clearly in one of two camps. Pro-choice legislators focus on the individual decision concerning a pregnancy, arguing that women should have the right to make their own decisions about reproductive issues in consultation with their doctors. The state should not intervene in what is best understood as a private decision. Pro-life advocates, on the other hand, focus less on the pregnant woman's decision-making process and instead argue that government has a duty to protect the life of the unborn child. From this perspective, the developing fetus is a human being with a right to life, so this right must be protected over the individual concerns of the mother. Pro-life legislators view abortion as murder and, therefore, cannot remain silent. Pro-choice advocates view abortion as a personal medical procedure and fear government intrusion on a woman's privacy rights.

Because the arguments on both sides of the abortion debate are firmly rooted in strongly held convictions about the beginning of human life, the dignity of and respect for women's decision making, and the proper role of government, legislators rarely find areas for compromise on this issue. Most activists for and against abortion rights agree with the goal of decreasing abortion rates, but they disagree fundamentally on how to achieve this end.

The safe-havens issue offered a rare moment for pro-choice and pro-life legislators to work together on a reproductive issue; no one wants to find a baby dead from exposure. Legislators on both sides of the abortion debate could find common ground working to prevent infant abandonment. An active proponent of the pro-life view, Hart thus welcomed the opportunity to promote legislation that could bridge the abortion divide and build consensus in one area where all seemed to agree: protecting newborns.

Can We All Get Along? Partisan Politics in the Contemporary Congress

Working across the aisle with members of the opposing political party is not a simple task in the current political environment. In recent decades, both the House and the Senate have become increasingly partisan. President Bill Clinton's impeachment is emblematic of the heightened partisan rancor. From Hillary Clinton's appearance on the *Today Show* deriding the impeachment as a "vast right-wing conspiracy" against her husband to the near party-line votes in the House and Senate, the impeachment was just the beginning of a new wave of public party warfare. The filibusters, stalemate, and showdowns over the Senate confirmation of President George W. Bush's most controversial judicial nominees offer even more examples of party politics paraded before the television cameras.

From hot debates in the national spotlight to the quieter passage of routine legislation, the roots of contemporary congressional party politics began in the restructuring of committees in the 1970s. Concerned about individual members wielding enough power to halt legislative action single-handedly, congressional reformers in the 1970s sought to reduce the power of committee chairs and in turn concentrated power within parties to encourage enactment of party programs. While the initial redirection of power and control to parties appeared to break certain forms of deadlock, this reform set the stage for the development of cohesive and ultimately divisive parties.[1] During and after the Reagan administration, **partisanship** continued to increase as parties and party leaders grew more ideologically homogeneous, in part because of Democrats' unifying to oppose Reagan's conservative agenda.

Although many sources help to create the partisan climate in Washington, one important contributing factor is party control of government institutions. A center of scholarly debate about political parties in the United States prominent in the 1960s and 1970s, **critical realignment theory**, posits that one of the two major political parties dominates American national politics for about a generation before losing power in a transformative election. History reveals a pattern of one party controlling the presidency, the House of Representatives, and the Senate for a span of about three decades, pursuing its agenda and shaping public policy. Then, in a sweeping revolt at the ballot box called a "critical realignment," the national mood abruptly shifts, and the voters usher in another party and a new political program. First discussed in the 1950s, if the theory held, a new era of party dominance should have begun sometime in the 1990s.[2]

Instead of solidifying political control for one party, however, the results of elections in recent decades have often split power between Republicans and Democrats, creating an era of **divided government**, with power shifting between the two major parties. For the past few decades, therefore, neither Democrats nor Republicans have been able to dominate political power in Washington. Unlike the anticipated traditional realignment in favor of one political party, the current pattern of partisan control is less stable, a trend that many observers call **dealignment**.

One factor that has contributed to this new political landscape is the change in patterns of partisanship in the South. The Democratic dominance of southern politics that began in the aftermath of the Civil War began to fade by the 1970s and 1980s. Many voters shifted their allegiances to the Republican Party, and some formerly Democratic elected officials switched parties. As Republicans gained strength in the South, the congressional delegation changed: "Between 1974 and 2004, the party breakdown of House members from the eleven former states of the confederacy reversed—from two-thirds Democrat to almost two-thirds Republican."[3] Regional patterns of representation transformed in the Senate as well with Republicans gaining many seats previously held by conservative Democrats. With these shifts, the Democrats lost their firm grip on control of the House of Representatives, and the margin in the Senate narrowed.

From the mid-1990s and into the George W. Bush era, the presidential margins of victory have often been small, and the margin of party control in both the House and the Senate is narrow and hard to hold together. Even when one party appears to dominate a chamber, the presence of moderate legislators in each party, slim margins of party control, and procedures such as the filibuster in the Senate combine to create a political reality that is far more complex.

Perhaps even more significant, however, the trend of almost even division between the two parties not only is found in federal elective offices but permeates the entire political system as well. Political observers like to talk about "red and blue" America, terms that allude to the electoral maps projected by the news media on Election Day to show the majority winner of the presidential vote in each state. "Red" states voted for the Republican candidate, and "blue" states signify a Democratic majority of electoral votes. Such color-coded maps do reveal interesting patterns, but they are not the most accurate portrayal of the depth of partisanship across the country. Because the election results in each state are often very close, it would probably be more accurate to describe most states as "purple"—mixtures of Republican and Democratic voters.

The current political era of divided government and relatively even party division across the states encourages high levels of partisanship. Simply put, narrow margins raise the stakes and discourage cooperation across party lines. Only a slight shift in voting could change party control of the presidency, House, or Senate; therefore, many party leaders believe that they need to claim all major policy victories for themselves and not risk sharing credit with their rivals as they await the next election.

PATTERNS OF PARTISANSHIP

To maintain control with such narrow margins, party discipline has increased as each party's leadership tries to rein in independent-minded legislators. From many vantage points, the discipline seems to be effective. Various measures of partisanship provide evidence of increased party cohesiveness in the past decade. For example, the average member of Congress votes with his or her party almost nine times out of ten.[4] One scholar measured partisanship levels in committee action, floor process, and presidential/congressional agreement on legislation and found consistent patterns of partisanship in every arena.[5] The data also reveal a rise in the ideological polarization between the two parties. In the late 1960s, for example, the parties shared more common ground, with many Democrats and Republicans sharing similar views on policy issues. Now the parties are much more ideologically distinct[6]—most Republicans are conservative, most Democrats are liberal, and the numbers of moderates in each party's congressional delegation seem to shrink with each election.

One common measure of partisanship in Congress is the percentage of **party unity votes**, those floor votes in which a majority of Republican legislators vote on the opposite side of a majority of their Democratic counterparts. For most congressional sessions between 1954 and 2002, less than half the House and Senate floor votes were party unity votes. The numbers increased for a few years in the mid-1980s and spiked during Bill Clinton's presidency, reaching a high point in 1995, the year after the Republicans won a majority in the House. That year, 73 percent of House votes and 69 percent of Senate votes pitted a majority of either party against the other. By the late 1990s, however, the party unity votes were back closer to the averages from the previous few decades.[7]

Although the percentage of polarized floor votes has remained reasonably steady over time, voting along party lines has increased in recent decades. In the 1970s, the percentages of Democrats and Republicans in both chambers that voted with their parties on party unity votes hovered around 75 percent. By 1985, however, House Democrats voted together on 86 percent and House Republicans on 80 percent of the chamber's party unity votes. By the 107th Congress (2001–2002), party cohesiveness was reaching near record highs, with about nine out of ten representatives and senators voting with their parties on these votes.[8]

Such partisan patterns can lead to gridlock. In a time of party parity during which defections by a few can change the outcome of a vote, the stakes grow even higher for legislators to follow their party's leadership. Narrow party margins lead to a perverse incentive structure: It appears to be better strategy to accomplish nothing and be able to cast blame squarely on the opposing party than to accomplish something but have to share political credit.

The trends of party dealignment and national party parity create a difficult political environment for legislators like Representative Hart who want to work with members of the opposing party. Working closely across party lines may raise suspicions; those who choose not to "toe the party line" face possible recriminations from within their chamber and even from the White House. For many in the current political climate, then, partisanship is the path of least resistance.

BRIDGING THE PARTISAN DIVIDE: BUILDING COALITIONS

In light of the trend toward increased partisanship in Congress, coalition building has become an even more important legislative tool. Political **coalitions** form across ideological and party lines, enabling legislators to build support for bills that might outwardly appear partisan and divisive. Coalition building in Congress offers one way to bridge the divide between parties, breaking down rather than building up barriers that prevent legislators from supporting certain legislative proposals.

Several factors contribute to the need for coalitions in Congress today. The structure of the House and Senate inherently increases the importance of building coalitions. Committees serve as the locus of House discussion, debate, and work on bills. However, cues from party leaders and inflammatory rhetoric tend to dominate committee decision outcomes and procedure more than political compromise does. Thus, legislators must rely on informal coalitions to help them work behind the scenes toward common goals during the many stages of bill writing and passage.

What political scientists call the dual nature of Congress creates other incentives for legislators to work in coalitions. At the same time that Congress serves as the lawmaking institution described in textbooks, debating and enacting legislation, it is also a body of elected officials who represent the specific needs and concerns of voters in their individual districts and states.[9] To be a successful representative or senator, then, a legislator must work within the institutional norms in Washington without losing sight of the voters' concerns. Coalitions form in part to help members respond to their constituents, providing a forum for working together with other like-minded legislators regardless of party affiliation.

Although congressional voting records show strong trends toward increased partisanship on Capitol Hill, legislators are not afraid to work against party goals if they believe an issue is in the best interests of the voters. A Democrat and a Republican from rural districts, for example, may find that their concern for farmers' interests is greater than their partisan ties. While the majority party leadership can provide the needed support to move many proposed bills, the party's power extends only so far. Ultimately, the voters decide if an incumbent legislator deserves reelection; therefore, most politicians give their first allegiance to their constituents.

Political freedom to vote across party lines depends, at least in part, on one's constituency. Political scientists distinguish between "safe" and "marginal" electoral districts; a **marginal seat** is typically defined as one in which the winner receives less than 55 or 60 percent of the vote in the last election; a **safe seat**, an election won with more than 60 percent of the vote, is assumed to be a guaranteed win for an incumbent seeking reelection. In an ironic twist, members from marginal districts often have more political freedom than members from safe districts. That is, if an incumbent expects a tight reelection, he or she will be freer to vote against the party; if a member is from a safe district, he or she faces even more pressure from leadership to toe the party line. Following this logic, then, legislators from competitive districts face fewer barriers to voting their conscience than those from safer seats.

Representative Hart was the first Republican elected to Congress from her district in more than three decades. If she needed to vote with her constituents and against party leadership or even the Bush administration, she could do so without too much fear of recrimination. Although she faced strong pressure to vote with Republicans, she also knew that the party would much prefer that she occasionally vote against them and remain in Congress than risk losing her seat to the Democrats in the next election.

Given the current stakes, members of Congress face the most difficulty trying to pass substantive legislation with bipartisan coalitions. Members will work across party lines to pass simple, noncontentious legislation, but they are less willing to share the credit on significant policy matters. At least in the current congressional climate, it appears that most bipartisan coalitions will pass primarily symbolic or uncontroversial bills. Hart's safe-havens proposal seemed to fit this description, so it would be reasonable to look for ways of partnering with Democrats on the bill.

SIGNING ON THE DOTTED LINE: BUILDING SUPPORT FOR LEGISLATION

Working in partnership with the other party may not be the current norm when addressing high-profile policy issues, but bipartisan cooperation is still the expected practice for many congressional actions. When introducing legislation, for example, most legislators look to their colleagues in the other party for help with building support.

SECURING COSPONSORS

The member who writes a bill and presents it before the chamber for consideration is identified as the **sponsor** of the bill. The sponsor serves as the primary spokesperson, cheerleader, and advocate for his or her legislation. Before officially introducing a bill, however, the sponsor enlists the support of others in the chamber, asking them to join the legislation as **cosponsors**. The clerks of the House and Senate record the name and date that each person signs on to a bill and, in the rare instance that a legislator has a change of heart, the date on which a person removes his or her name from the list. Cosponsorship is a public pronouncement of strong support for a bill, so sponsors typically seek to add as many legislators as possible to a proposal in order to gain more leverage for moving it through the legislative process. The greater the number of cosponsors on a bill, the greater the pressure on party and committee leaders to act.

Although the sponsor and cosponsors are always free to vote as they choose if a given measure reaches the floor for a vote, their willingness to attach their names to a bill is a very strong indicator that they will vote for the legislation. An occasional member will admit to cosponsoring a bill only to make a political point and with no intention of voting in favor of the bill if it did come to the floor, but such antics are rare. Cosponsorship thus sends an important signal to constituents, interest-group leaders, and lobbyists who support a particular bill. When lobbyists meet with legislators, for example, they often ask them to cosponsor legislation, knowing that such an action all but guarantees the member will support the bill in committee and on the floor. Legislators, in turn, who are unsure about or want to minimize their public identification with a proposal may avoid signing on to a bill. Cosponsorship makes friends, but it also makes enemies. Wise members will be selective in the number and subject matter of bills to which they lend such strong public support.

The process of securing cosponsors builds in several stages. Before officially introducing a bill, the sponsor solicits a **primary cosponsor**, often a person from the opposite party who will agree to champion the legislation among fellow partisans. Once a primary cosponsor has agreed to join the bill, that legislator joins the sponsor in enlisting help from other members. Those who agree to sign on to a bill before its official introduction are called **original cosponsors**, a status that signifies early and fervent support for the proposal. When the new bill is entered into the congressional record, the text of the bill will include the names of the sponsor and primary cosponsor followed by the others who added their names to the legislation before its introduction.

FINDING THE LEAD DEMOCRATIC COSPONSOR

Once Representative Hart had a working draft of the Safe Havens Support Act, she began the process of finding the initial Democrat who would join her on the bill. First and foremost, she wanted to find someone who shared her concern about the problem of infant abandonment. To demonstrate that this bill was important to those on both sides of the abortion debate, Hart hoped to partner with a pro-choice member to balance her pro-life stance. Finally, she sought a colleague with a good reputation in the chamber, a strong and capable staff, and access to new networks of legislators who could be persuaded to join the bill.

The search led to Representative Stephanie Tubbs Jones, a second-term Democrat from Cleveland, Ohio. The process began by identifying Democrats who had cosponsored related legislation in past Congresses. Tubbs Jones was an original cosponsor of the Child Abuse Prevention and Enforcement Act and was one of only three Democrats in the 106th Congress that cosponsored H. Res. 465, asking officials at all levels of government to keep statistics relating to infant abandonment. Her track record supporting these bills indicated her interest in the issue and suggested her willingness to work with Republicans.

Although she was among the more liberal Democrats in the chamber, Tubbs Jones was also known as a team player who sought opportunities for bipartisan cooperation. Her background as an attorney, former judge, and former prosecutor gave her added credibility to talk about safe-havens programs. She understood the legal issues at stake and would be able to speak directly to the legal professionals who were working to reduce infant abandonment. As an active member of the Congressional Black Caucus, Tubbs Jones could also build support for safe havens within this important network of Democratic legislators.

With Tubbs Jones identified as the preferred Democratic cosponsor, conversations between the two offices' staff members and between the two representatives began. Tubbs Jones's office expressed a strong interest in the Safe Havens Support Act at the initial contact. Hart had secured Tubbs Jones's agreement to join the bill in only a matter of hours after describing the purposes of the bill and forwarding the legislative director the latest draft from the Office of Legislative Counsel. With the primary Democratic cosponsor now in place, the Hart-Tubbs Jones Safe Havens Support Act was moving closer to introduction in the House.

CIRCULATING "DEAR COLLEAGUE" LETTERS

Legislators use a variety of techniques to build interest in and support for their proposals. One of the most popular methods for soliciting cosponsors is circulating requests known as **dear colleague letters**. The most common of these communications is a generic letter sent to all members of the chamber briefly describing a bill, what it proposes to accomplish, and why a member should join the cause. The letter ends with a plea for a vote or a request for cosponsors and includes contact information for the legislative staff responsible for the bill. Copied in bulk and distributed through the internal mail, the letters typically begin with the generic salutation "Dear Colleague." Offices receive these letters along with hundreds of other internal and external communications that arrive in the mail each day. Although the protocol for responding to these requests varies for different offices, all legislative staffs have a system for alerting the member about requests for cosponsorship and soliciting feedback.

Mass mailings to every person in a chamber are the most common form of dear colleagues, but legislators can tailor these communications to a group as large or as small as they choose. Members may send targeted letters to all of their fellow partisans, to members of their state delegations, or to any other affinity group that might be persuaded to sign on to the bill.

When gathering cosponsors for the Safe Havens Support Act, the two sponsors and their staffs circulated several dear colleague letters soliciting help. We tailored a few letters to particular groups, such as a letter from Representative Hart to everyone in her "freshman class," those legislators who had entered the chamber in the 107th Congress. The day after the *Washington Post* ran a front-page story about two Virginia college students facing criminal charges for the abandonment and subsequent death of their newborn baby, Hart circulated a copy of the article with a letter beginning, "Perhaps you read the front-page story in Sunday's *Washington Post* about the Virginia college student who hid her pregnancy from her family, gave birth to a healthy baby girl, and abandoned her newborn daughter in a portable toilet at a Delaware construction site." The letter told of the work of safe-havens programs to combat infant abandonment and invited colleagues to join Hart's bill as original cosponsors. After Tubbs Jones joined the bill, she and Hart circulated a letter to everyone in the chamber that included headlines from articles in five newspapers across the country lauding safe-havens programs. Figure 6.1 shows a copy of this dear colleague letter. As the number of Republican and Democratic cosponsors grew, we sent updated letters to everyone in the chamber with a list of all the current supporters of the bill.

CAPITALIZING ON CAUCUS CONNECTIONS

Congressional membership organizations (CMOs), those groups of members described in chapter 3, also play an important role in building support for a bill. From the Congressional Ski and Snowboard Caucus to the Steel Caucus and everything in between, groups of legislators meet together, share ideas, and plan legislative strategy on the basis of their common interests.

Just as Representative Hart found assistance from CMOs in the early stages of writing the Safe Havens Support Act, so did she turn to several caucuses to build support for the final bill. Hart is a member of the Republican Study Committee (RSC), a caucus of conservative, family-values Republicans whose members meet weekly for a lunchtime discussion of political strategy. At these weekly meetings, individuals request time to address the group, looking for support for their legislation. In the weeks before introducing the Safe Havens Support Act, Hart used a weekly RSC meeting to build support. She described her bill and passed a sign-up sheet around the table so that interested members could join as original cosponsors of the bill. Eight members not already helping with the bill added their support. Most requests for support reach members more slowly through the filter of their legislative staff; in this meeting, Hart was able to lobby her colleagues directly and get instant commitments of cosponsorship.

The congresswoman also sought support from the Values Action Team (VAT), a group of socially conservative members. VAT hosts two weekly meetings. Weekly lunches for designated representatives from VAT members' offices provide a forum for updating staff on legislation of interest that is working its way through committees or onto the floor. Those in attendance also have an opportunity to describe any bills their bosses are working on

FIGURE 6.1: SAFE HAVENS DEAR COLLEAGUE LETTER

Help Prevent the Abandonment and Death of Infants:
Become an Original Co-Sponsor of the Safe Havens Support Act

Dear Colleague,

Perhaps you read the front-page story in Sunday's *Washington Post* about the Virginia college student who hid her pregnancy from her family, gave birth to a healthy baby girl, and then abandoned her newborn daughter in a portable toilet at a Delaware construction site. And how can we forget the story of the teenager in New Jersey who delivered a baby in a restroom, abandoned the child in a trash can, and returned to her high school prom? Or perhaps you recall the report this spring of an abandoned infant discovered in a backyard mauled by a hungry dog?

Stories of parents in crisis who abandon newborn babies are all too commonplace. It is impossible to know the exact number of infants abandoned each year, but media accounts remind us that this is a growing problem nationwide. Between 1991 and 1998, for example, media reports of the number of abandoned babies discovered nationwide almost doubled.

In response to this growing problem, twenty-five states have passed safe havens laws, legislation that encourages responsible behavior by individuals unwilling or unable to care for their babies. Under these provisions, a parent can relinquish an unharmed infant to caregivers at designated locations, avoid prosecution, and save their baby's life.

Although the states are reacting quickly and decisively to the problem of infant abandonment, it is clear that states need assistance from the federal government to make these laws work effectively. For example, early reports from states with safe havens laws suggest that the laws have little impact on the problem without coordinated publicity campaigns. The Safe Havens Support Act will help state and local baby abandonment programs promote their services, reach those in crisis who are at greatest risk of abandoning their babies, and provide the training and technical assistance to help save babies' lives.

We do not know enough about the characteristics of women who abandon their babies, nor do we know enough about the scope nor the extent of the problem. This legislation will also mandate a Department of Health and Human Resources study to increase our understanding of how and why this happens so we can prevent women from reaching this crisis point in the first place.

I urge you to join me in supporting this legislation to help promote safe havens programs across the country. To become an original co-sponsor or to learn more about this important legislation, call Amy Black or Bill Rys at 5-2565.

Yours very truly,

Melissa A. Hart
Member of Congress

Source: Office of Congresswoman Melissa A. Hart (PA-04).

WINNING FRIENDS TO INFLUENCE PEOPLE

and to distribute dear colleagues soliciting more support. Each Thursday that Congress is in session, VAT also convenes meetings with representatives from interest groups who share related goals and issue concerns. In these sessions, the groups inform one another about their recent work and devise political strategy. Hart's office presented the Safe Havens Support Act in both of these meetings. As the legislative assistant assigned to VAT, I discussed the bill and circulated a dear colleague at the staff meeting, and Representative Hart briefed the interest-group leaders on the bill.

As Hart was building support within her networks, Representative Tubbs Jones was also working to add cosponsors to the bill. She approached Democratic members of the Education and Workforce Committee and members of the Congressional Black Caucus to support the legislation, encouraging several to join the bill. Together, Hart and Tubbs Jones worked with the bipartisan Congressional Caucus for Women's Issues to build interest in safe havens. Eventually, the women's caucus included H.R. 2018 on its list of bills to support, and seventeen of its members cosponsored the legislation.

PERSONAL LOBBYING

Circulating internal mail and presenting legislation in caucus meetings are important ways to build support for legislation, but perhaps nothing is more effective than direct lobbying from member to member. On the floor of the House, in the congressional dining room, or even in the elevator on the way to a vote, legislators chat informally with one another and solicit support for current projects and legislation. Hart and Tubbs Jones were successful in both personally lobbying colleagues and encouraging them to cosponsor their bill.

LETTERS OF SUPPORT FROM OUTSIDE GROUPS

Interest groups, charities, and trade associations are additional sources of support for legislation. If an outside group agrees with a legislative proposal and wants to see it passed, a leader of the organization may write a public letter of support praising the bill that the sponsor can circulate to other members and to the media. Groups may also help by activating their membership to lobby their legislators, publicizing a bill in the organization's communications, or persuading other lobbyists to join the coalition supporting the measure.

Hart's chief of staff, Bill Ries, developed an outreach plan for encouraging outside groups to back the Safe Havens Support Act. Within a few months of introducing the bill, he had secured letters from organizations as diverse as the National Right to Life Committee, the American Medical Association, and Catholic Charities. In general, the smaller organizations offered quick feedback; larger, national organizations often had to wait for months as the request worked its way through approval processes.

Requesting help from outside organizations incurs some risk. Although members and their aides work to identify likely supporters, some groups that appear friendly may, in practice, oppose the bill. Building strong communications networks with congressional staff and organization leaders can provide inside information to identify whether groups are likely friends or foes, but even the best networking has limits.

With H.R. 2018, we found hostility from an unlikely source, the Family Research Council (FRC). A member of the outside coalition group of the Values Action Team known for its work on "pro-family" issues, the FRC seemed to be a perfect fit for the safe-havens bill. By the time that Hart introduced the Safe Havens Support Act, however, the FRC had begun some preliminary research into infant-abandonment laws and expressed reservations about them. Their discussion memo on the topic raised concern about the unintended consequences of safe-havens laws, noting that they "appear to accept [the] idea of baby abandonment—even making it acceptable." The memo concluded with a series of bullet points, with the final statement arguing, "The state appears to be following the abnormal and undesirable practices of some mothers, enshrining such actions as 'policy.'... Problems arise when policy is made to accommodate the deviant. It usually ends up encouraging the deviant more than anything else."[10] By asking the FRC to support Hart's bill, we had unknowingly alerted a potential opponent of pending legislation. At this point, the strategy changed from seeking the FRC's support to trying to minimize potential damage along with providing information and new data that would help assuage their concerns.

PARTY LEADERSHIP

Party leaders are another potential source of help when building momentum in favor of legislation. The **Speaker of the House** is the most powerful and visible person in Congress. Members of the House of Representatives convene at the beginning of each new Congress to elect the Speaker. Although each party nominates its own candidate for the speakership, the majority party's candidate always wins. The Speaker officially presides over business in the chamber; in practice, however, other members share the duties at the rostrum. In addition to serving as the head of the majority party in the House, the Speaker's duties include setting the agenda for floor business, keeping party members in line with the leadership's goals, influencing the committee assignment process, appointing members to conference committees, and serving as an official spokesperson with the media.

The Constitution assigns the vice president the role of presiding officer of the Senate. In the absence of the vice president, the **president pro-tempore**, the longest-serving member of the majority party, assumes this authority. As in the House, senators share responsibility for presiding over the day-to-day business in the chamber, with select senators from the majority party taking turns at the rostrum during normal legislative business.

Party leaders have important roles in both chambers, helping to keep their party on message and guiding the legislative agenda. The party with the most members in the normal legislative chamber elects the **majority leader**. In the House, the majority leader handles much of the daily work of scheduling and moving legislation through the chamber, working in concert with the Speaker. The **minority leader** presents the case of the opposition party, identifies weaknesses in policies supported by the majority party, and presents alternative policy plans.

As the highest-ranking party leader in the Senate, the majority leader is the primary spokesperson for the party and its programs. Although ultimately responsible for scheduling activity on the Senate floor, in practice most majority leaders work with the minority leader to plan major legislative activities.

Each party also elects **whips**, leaders given the responsibility of mobilizing votes and disseminating information to fellow partisans. The term "whip" comes from "whipper-in," a fox-hunting term for the person charged with keeping dogs from straying during a chase.[11] Each party's whip heads the entire whip organization, a group of members assigned to help persuade other legislators to vote with the party. Whips will use a variety of persuasive techniques to build support for important measures. The whip's office also keeps track of how members are planning to vote, running so-called whip counts to see if they have sufficient votes to pass (or defeat) proposals on the floor.

Perhaps the most important daily task of the party whip is communicating information. The office keeps an updated schedule of upcoming floor activity and expected votes. When members or senators have events and meetings away from Capitol Hill, the whip's office helps them know when they will be expected on the floor for a vote. The whip also provides information about the content of pending legislation as well as the party's position on issues coming before the chamber for a vote.

A final component of the party organization is the conference or caucus (the latter term preferred by House Democrats), the group of all the Republicans or all the Democrats in each chamber. The primary vehicle for communicating the party message, **party caucuses** meet weekly when Congress is in session to share information from party leadership, debate issues, and plan strategy. Before the beginning of each new Congress, these groups convene to elect new party leaders.[12]

Hart's office worked with party leadership to build momentum for the Safe Havens Support Act. The most direct help came from the office of then–majority whip Tom DeLay. In an important gesture, DeLay agreed to cosponsor H.R. 2018. One of his legislative aides had worked previously as the staff director for the Human Resources Subcommittee of Ways and Means, so she understood the safe-havens issue and child welfare legislation moving through Congress. In the months following introduction of the bill, DeLay's staff served as a great resource, providing inside information to help with political strategy and working behind the scenes to move the bill.

Although Speaker of the House Dennis Hastert cosponsors legislation only on rare occasions, his policy staff promised to help if Hart needed aid with moving the bill in committee. Armed with assurances of assistance behind the scenes, Hart moved forward with great confidence.

In the final analysis, the personal lobbying, meetings with caucuses and interest groups, and distribution of dear colleague letters worked. Seventy-six representatives from both ends of the ideological spectrum cosponsored the Safe Havens Support Act. With such a solid base of bipartisan support in place, Hart was finally ready to introduce H.R. 2018, the Safe Havens Support Act.

CHAPTER SUMMARY

The current political environment in Congress is very partisan. In recent decades, control of the House of Representatives, the Senate, and the presidency has shifted between Republicans and Democrats, creating an era of divided government. Narrow margins of party control discourage cooperation across party lines and increase political pressure for legislators to vote with their party leadership.

Coalition building is an important tool for bridging the partisan divide in Congress. Before introducing a bill, most legislators ask a member of the other party to cosponsor the measure. Hart found such help from Representative Stephanie Tubbs Jones, a Democrat from Ohio who helped build a diverse, bipartisan network of cosponsors. The two members together circulated dear colleague letters to everyone in the chamber and individually built networks of support with caucuses and outside groups.

NOTES

1. For a more comprehensive discussion of these reforms, see David W. Rohde, *Parties and Leaders in the Postreform House* (Chicago: University of Chicago Press, 1991).
2. See, e.g., V. O. Key Jr., "A Theory of Critical Elections," *Journal of Politics* 17 no. 1 (February 1955): 3–18; Walter Dean Burnham, *Critical Elections and the Mainsprings of American Politics* (New York: W. W. Norton, 1970).
3. Jacob Hacker and Paul Pierson, *Off Center: The Republican Revolution and the Erosion of American Democracy* (New Haven, Conn.: Yale University Press, 2005), 117.
4. Roger H. Davidson and Walter J. Oleszek, *Congress and Its Members*, 9th ed. (Washington, D.C.: Congressional Quarterly Press, 2004), 273.
5. Barbara Sinclair, "Hostile Partners: The President, Congress, and Lawmaking in the Partisan 1990s," in *Polarized Politics: Congress and the President in a Partisan Era*, ed. Jon R. Bond and Richard Fleisher (Washington, D.C.: Congressional Quarterly Press, 2000), 137–40.

6. Sarah A. Binder, *Stalemate: Causes and Consequences of Legislative Gridlock* (Washington, D.C.: Brookings Institution Press, 2003), 23–25.
7. Harold W. Stanley and Richard G. Niemi, *Vital Statistics on American Politics 2003–2004* (Washington, D.C.: Congressional Quarterly Press, 2003), 216.
8. Ibid., 217.
9. Davidson and Oleszek, 4–5.
10. "Infant Abandonment Laws: FRC Discussion Memo" (Washington, D.C.: Family Research Council, undated memo), 12.
11. James Q. Wilson and John J. DiIluio Jr., *American Government: The Essentials*, 9th ed. (Boston: Houghton Mifflin, 2004), 298.
12. For more information about the role and function of party leaders, see Davidson and Oleszek, chapter 6.

LIGHTS, CAMERA, ACTION!

DEVELOPING MEDIA STRATEGY

Representative Hart and her legislative staff devoted months of effort to researching the issue of infant abandonment, designing and crafting a proposal, and mobilizing other members to cosponsor safe-havens legislation. Although all these efforts were necessary to create a strong network of support on Capitol Hill, this work alone was not sufficient to maximize the likelihood that safe-havens legislation would succeed. Hart also needed to design a media strategy that could raise awareness of the issue and direct attention to her work. Media coverage could inform constituents and build even more momentum to propel her safe-havens proposal forward in the legislative process.

Exploring some of the reasons why successful politicians must develop a media strategy for communicating their concerns to voters and the press, this chapter examines the relationship between members of Congress and the news media. Next, it considers patterns of local and national media coverage of Congress and introduces some of the most common tools that politicians use to communicate with voters and the media. Finally, the chapter examines a few of Hart's successes and failures as she sought to raise public awareness of the problem of infant abandonment and her proposed legislation.

THE NEWS MEDIA: PERVASIVE AND IMPORTANT

Almost all Americans look to the news media as their primary source of information about politics and current events. Few voters have direct and sustained contact with members of Congress, so various media outlets serve as their primary sources of information about elected officials and their achievements. Even those who want to avoid technology likely glean most of their political knowledge from the media, learning secondhand from family and friends about events and policies reported in the news. Even elites turn to print, broadcast, and electronic sources for politically relevant information. As one media scholar summarizes, "The ability to attract such vast audiences of ordinary people, as well as political elites, constitutes a major ingredient in the power of the mass media and makes them extraordinarily important for the individuals and groups whose stories and causes are publicized."[1]

In this media-saturated age, it is no surprise that members of Congress devote time and effort to developing and promoting strategies for maximizing positive press coverage. Candidates for office can expect a few journalists to report on their campaigns, but once in office legislators struggle to attract media coverage of their daily work. Representative David Price describes this problem: "Members of the media, especially television, are often attracted to campaign fireworks, but it takes considerably more effort to interest them in the day-to-day work of Congress."[2]

WORKING FROM BOTH ENDS: ATTRACTING LOCAL AND NATIONAL NEWS COVERAGE

Because legislators divide their time between midweek work in Washington and frequent trips back home for long weekends of constituent events, those seeking media coverage need to communicate with both national and local news organizations. When in Washington, members of Congress and their press aides focus most attention on those journalists assigned to cover Congress; when working back home, members seek press coverage from a wide array of broadcast and print sources in the various localities scattered across the district. Both sources of media serve legislators' goals. Those who want to maintain a vibrant presence with their constituents court local media coverage; those who want to build their reputations as policy experts need to attract the attention of reporters based in Washington.

NATIONAL MEDIA COVERAGE OF CONGRESS

Many news organizations assign reporters to particular **beats**, categories of news events that they follow and report. Some journalists work substantive beats covering a particular subject, such as the environment or religion; others receive beat assignments for a particular location, such as the Pentagon or the White House. To encourage coverage of daily legislative business, members of Congress will likely find it most advantageous to build relationships with journalists assigned the congressional beat. When seeking to raise awareness of a legislative proposal, however, legislators will also want to pitch stories to reporters who cover substantive beats.

Even though some journalists are assigned to cover Congress, the institution and its members receive far less media attention than does the president.

Several factors likely contribute to the imbalance in coverage. Widely described as the most powerful leader in the free world, the president naturally commands media attention. In addition, reporters find it easier to cover the White House than Congress. Fed with daily press briefings and allotted space in a designated press wing in the basement of the White House, reporters assigned to cover the president have easy access to information and prepackaged news stories every day.

The reporters who cover Congress, on the other hand, have the unenviable task of monitoring the actions of 435 members of the House and 100 senators, scores of committees and subcommittees, and thousands of legislative proposals. Adding difficulty to the journalists' task, news editors and producers often assume that the average reader or viewer will be less interested in the intricate details of the legislative process than the actions of one well-known and easily identified individual, the president. Given these complexities, journalists and the members they cover must work creatively to get time and space in national media stories.

Aware of the ongoing battle to attract national media coverage, Hart's staff actively cultivate working relationships with reporters who cover Congress. To facilitate building connections, Hart's press secretary compiled a twenty-page media guide listing names and contact information for journalists from a wide range of media outlets. Updated regularly, the list includes dozens of reporters, editors, and bureau chiefs from wire services, national newspapers, magazines, and Washington publications. Anytime that Hart wants to raise national awareness of an issue or bill, her press secretary can contact journalists listed in the media guide and update them on the congresswoman's recent activity.

PATTERNS OF LOCAL COVERAGE
OF MEMBERS OF CONGRESS

Anecdotal evidence suggests that members of Congress vary in their success at capturing attention in local media outlets, but few researchers have investigated patterns of local news coverage of members of Congress. A study of media reports on routine Senate votes found that daily newspapers rarely report voting results unless the issue seems "politically important"; senators who voted contrary to expectations were most likely to receive coverage.[3] The most comprehensive local media study to date finds that stories about members of Congress "[take] up a small but regular slice of local news space."[4] The researcher identifies three factors that contribute to the quality and quantity of local press coverage of Congress: individual characteristics of different media formats, members' relationships with journalists, and the overlap between a member's legislative district and the media markets.[5]

Certain media formats lend themselves more readily to coverage of elected officials. Weekly newspapers and evening newscasts often need to fill space, so these venues may highlight a legislator's local activities, especially if accompanied by good visuals and easy sound bites. Coverage will also reflect, in part, the quality of the relationships between the member, his or her press aides, and the journalists. Members who build positive working relationships with local journalists are more likely to generate press coverage than those who refuse to return phone calls. A third factor, congruence with media markets, also affects how much local press a legislator receives. Congressional districts can stretch across hundreds of miles and scores of towns and small cities, or they may be compact, densely populated slices of a major metropolitan area. Sprawling districts may include several newspapers and multiple **broadcast markets**; members from compact urban districts may compete for media attention with five, ten, or more representatives with districts served by the same local television stations. The final analysis suggests that the tighter the overlap between a legislative district and media outlets, the greater the likelihood that the member will receive local news coverage.[6]

Hart's congressional district extends across five counties, wrapping around the city of Pittsburgh and continuing westward to the Ohio border. Although her district includes small cities and rural areas, many of the district's residents live within the Pittsburgh media market. Comprising the twenty-second largest broadcast media market in the nation, Pittsburgh television stations reach an estimated 1.2 million viewers.[7] The largest newspaper in the area, the *Pittsburgh Post-Gazette*, claims an average daily circulation of 238,860.[8] The next largest paper, the *Pittsburgh Tribune Review*, together with its sibling the *Greensburg Tribune Review*, competes for Pittsburgh area readership and reaches an estimated 118,000 households daily.[9] When seeking coverage in the Pittsburgh media, the congresswoman vies for attention from the members representing the neighboring fourteenth and eighteenth districts, which are more centrally located within this market. Constituents in the western part of the district are part of a different and smaller broadcast market, one that is based in Youngstown, Ohio, and reaches an estimated 275,000 viewers in Ohio and parts of Pennsylvania.[10]

All told, most of Hart's district includes areas served by two different television broadcast markets, eight weekly newspapers, and ten daily newspapers. With so many media outlets scattered across her district that serve some of her constituents, Hart had to develop a complex media outreach plan to compete for press coverage.

MEDIA STRATEGY: CAPTURING PUBLIC ATTENTION

Legislators want to communicate effectively with their constituents, so they design media strategy that maximizes their ability to capture public attention. Every House and Senate office will include at least one staff member dedicated to handling the press; most Senate staffs include a small team of communications professionals. The person who coordinates media operations, usually called the **press secretary** or **communications director**, works actively to maximize both the quantity and the quality of media coverage.

Most members and senators hope that media coverage will increase their visibility, intending to boost their name recognition with potential voters. Some legislators have even loftier goals for their communications. Described as "**media entrepreneurs**," these politicians actively cultivate media opportunities to promote policy goals, seeking the attention of media outlets that are most likely to influence elite opinion.[11] As one scholar describes, "Across the board, media entrepreneurs consider the media an effective policy tool. . . . They consider the policy process and legislative machinery more permeable to the media's influences than their counterparts."[12]

Press secretaries distinguish two broad categories of media coverage: reactive and proactive. A legislator is in a reactive mode when responding to media inquiries. Some such stories can provide positive coverage, as when a local newspaper reporter asks the representative to explain her views on a bill she sponsored. Reactive stories all too often result in negative coverage, however, as in those cases when reporters are investigating allegations of misconduct or scandal. By contrast, a legislator in a proactive mode initiates media coverage and thus maintains a level of control over the content and agenda. The subjects of news stories cannot choose what a journalist will report, but they can design media opportunities that offer prepackaged visuals and snappy sound bites with the hope of generating positive coverage. Reporters under pressure to prepare stories quickly are often eager to incorporate the media-ready content.

NEWS HOOKS

Many politicians and their communications staff court media attention by looking for **news hooks**, stories from recent and breaking news that could be connected, or hooked, to a policy or activity they want to promote. As one media adviser explained in a guide for activists, "If a major story has broken in the national news media about your cause—or there is an ongoing national debate about it—local and national news outlets may be looking for 'local angles' about the story."[13]

Tragic events may provide excellent news hooks. For instance, an aide in one of Hart's district offices faxed the congresswoman a local newspaper report of an abandoned baby found dead in a wooded area of Ellwood City, Pennsylvania.[14] Greatly distressed that legislation was not yet in place to aid in the prevention of such a tragedy, Hart spoke with local media to raise awareness of the one safe-havens program in nearby Pittsburgh, to encourage parents in crisis not to abandon a newborn, and to plead for quick passage of safe-havens legislation in Pennsylvania and in the nation's capital.

THE BEST DEFENSE IS A GOOD OFFENSE

Even though media-savvy legislators recognize the importance of both reactive and proactive media, they create proactive media strategies to maximize positive news coverage. When working for a member of Congress or a senator, aides cultivate contacts with print and broadcast reporters both in the home district or state and in Washington. These introductions serve the interests of reporters and politicians; journalists know whom to contact when they need a quick quote or reaction, and press secretaries build networks for pitching future story ideas and sharing information.

Legislators also need to build connections with their constituents. Frequent communication and high visibility can build name recognition and may increase popularity with voters. Although media coverage builds credibility, members of Congress also want to connect directly with their constituents to maintain complete control over the content and tone of their communication.

Hart and her staff developed a proactive media strategy designed to promote safe havens and capture as much and as diverse of media coverage as possible. Specifically, we wanted to increase the visibility of the abandoned-infants problem to raise awareness of the issue and to build support for programs intended to prevent such tragedies. The congresswoman also hoped to educate the public about existing local safe-havens programs already in place. Shining a media spotlight on the work of A Hand to Hold and other similar organizations would increase the likelihood that mothers in crisis would learn about this lifesaving option. To accomplish these goals, the press secretary began networking with local and national journalists. A case study of two press conferences presented later in this chapter offers an insider's view of two of Hart's media outreach efforts.

TOOLS OF THE COMMUNICATIONS TRADE

Members of Congress and senators have many tools for communicating with their constituents and the news media.

INTERNET WEB SITES

Perhaps the most basic form of communication in the Internet age is an effective Web site. All members and senators receive space connected to the official House of Representatives and Senate government Web sites. Varying in comprehensiveness and style, most Web sites include a biography of the member or senator, photos, legislative activities and issue positions, text of news releases and speeches, and contact information. More sophisticated sites may link to video and audio clips; some even include a special section just for children. Web sites give legislators the opportunity to present themselves and their work directly to their constituents.

Hart and her staff recognized the importance of connecting with constituents online, so they devoted time and resources to creating an accessible and attractive Web site. In addition to the traditional sections common to most Web sites, Hart included an "Outreach Calendar" listing events scheduled in Washington and in the district and highlighting the fast pace of a legislator's schedule. The efforts to build an effective site paid off: an independent research project evaluating the Internet communications efforts of members of Congress awarded Hart's Web site its highest honors: the "gold mouse award."[15]

CONSTITUENT NEWSLETTERS

The rules of each chamber dictate specifics for how often and in what form representatives and senators can mail **constituent newsletters** to every household in their district or state. Typically sent about twice a year, these mailings update constituents on recent legislation, government programs that may be of interest, upcoming meetings in the district, and any other issues the legislator chooses to highlight. Rarely discussing policy with much detail, constituent newsletters build visibility and remind voters who is serving them in Washington.

Hart wanted to communicate with constituents more frequently, so she created an e-mail newsletter. Unlike traditional newsletters that are sent via postal mail and reach every household in the district, Hart sends her "Eye on Washington" update every week that Congress is in session to an e-mail list of subscribers. Each newsletter includes a section titled "Week in Review" that describes some of Hart's meetings, mentions awards, and lists new government services available in the district. Other sections, such as "Committee News" and "Events in the Fourth District," offer further updates on the congresswoman's work in Washington and Pennsylvania.

PRESS RELEASES

The primary tool of the press secretary's trade is the **press release**, a prefabricated news story distributed to the media for their use. Reporters are free to incorporate phrases, sentences, or even the entire text of a news release into their stories. Written in simple prose and punctuated with clever quotations, releases describe an event, a policy, or anything else the legislator hopes that the media will report. Most legislators have fax machines programmed to send press releases to every media outlet in the district at the touch of a button; some offices send releases daily.

The format of press releases can vary, but most include common elements. The top of a release includes the date and contact information for a person available to answer questions and provide further information. Most begin with a title that resembles a newspaper headline, and paragraphs are typically short.

Releases from elected officials are often replete with direct quotes—statements attributed to the politician ready for insertion into news stories. A signal on the final line such as "-30-" or "###" designates the official end of the text.

FIGURE 7.1: SAMPLE PRESS RELEASE

Hart Appointed To Powerful Ways And Means Committee

January 6, 2005

Lee Cohen

Press Secretary

WASHINGTON—U.S. Congresswoman Melissa Hart (PA-04) last night won a seat on the House Ways and Means Committee, one of the U.S. House's most powerful committees, and a highly coveted seat. The Ways and Means Committee has jurisdiction over taxes, Social Security, Medicare, and over the authority of the Federal Government to borrow money.

"I am pleased and honored to have been selected to serve on the Ways and Means Committee," said Hart. "This new committee appointment gives me an even greater opportunity to work on the issues critical to Western Pennsylvanians, particularly strengthening Social Security, improving Medicare, reforming taxes, and reducing the public debt." Hart added: "I'm looking forward to working with Chairman Thomas and my colleagues, including veteran Ways and Means Committee member, and fellow Pennsylvania Congressman Phil English."

The House Republican Steering Committee last night voted for Hart as one of five new Republican Members on the Ways and Means Committee for the 109th Congress. Hart will serve on the Subcommittee on Human Resources, which considers matters involving welfare reform, supplemental security income, aid to families with dependent children, social services, child support, eligibility of welfare recipients for food stamps, and low-income energy assistance. Hart will also serve on the Select Revenue Measures Subcommittee, which will consider revenue items on a case-by-case basis at the referral of the Chairman of the Committee.

"I'm very pleased that Congresswoman Hart will join the Ways and Means Committee. Melissa's work on tax and pension policy in the Pennsylvania State Senate and the leadership she has exhibited in the U.S. House will allow her to quickly add to the Committee's deliberation. We depend upon the Ways and Means Committee to help us to move our agenda, and I'm confident that Melissa Hart will help us achieve our goals to strengthen social security, to keep taxes low, to create jobs and grow the economy, and to work to make health care more accessible and affordable for Americans," said Speaker of the House J. Dennis Hastert.

Source: Office of Congresswoman Melissa A. Hart (PA-04).

Ideally, press aides would like to see journalists publish unaltered news releases as their stories. Data from studies of media coverage of Congress suggest that this is not very common. Although some papers do publish stories based exclusively or almost entirely on a news release, reporters ignore most releases sent to them. When papers or news stations do report a story that was introduced first in a press release, they may or may not quote from the prepackaged text.[16] Even if the resulting story goes in a different direction than the original news release, the press secretary will have accomplished an important goal: proactively creating interest in a particular subject or event.

OP-EDS

Another important form of communication for members of Congress is the opinion column or editorial, commonly called an "op-ed" piece. Most major daily newspapers and television news broadcasts aspire to the norm of objectivity, reporting news events without discernible bias or spin. Media outlets call such stories "**straight news**." When journalists openly express opinions, they refer to such subjective reports as "**editorials**." Daily newspapers often devote two pages in the back of the front section to these stories. In the left-hand column, members of the paper's editorial board offer their opinions on major issues of the day in unsigned essays. Newspapers gain reputations for the political slant of their editorial pages; the *New York Times* and the *Washington Post* are known for their liberal perspective, whereas the *Wall Street Journal* and the *Chicago Tribune* are more conservative.[17]

The remainder of the editorial/opinion section includes opinion essays from regular and guest contributors. Some newspapers have sufficient budgets to employ their own columnists, but most papers subscribe to **syndicated columns**, that is, essays by a specific writer replicated in various papers each day or week. Readers quickly learn the political leaning of prominent columnists; Paul Krugman and Molly Ivins are two noted liberal writers, whereas Robert Novak and William Safire offer a conservative spin on the issues. Editorial and opinion pages also include guest columns, often opinion essays on various topics written by academics, political leaders, and other experts. Legislators who hope to spotlight their favorite initiatives may submit **guest editorials** to newspapers. In these essays, politicians (or their aides, writing on their behalf) express their opinions on upcoming legislation or policy issues linked to current events. Guest editorials are an important form of direct communication with voters and opinion leaders, as these pieces give legislators a forum for explaining their views in much more detail than the typical short quote or sound bite reported in a straight news story.

LETTERS TO THE EDITOR

Sharing space with the opinion columns in the editorial/opinion section, **letters to the editor** provide readers an opportunity to express their own views in the form of correspondence with the newspaper. Members of the editorial staff read incoming mail and select a handful of letters to edit and print in the paper each day.

Savvy politicians make use of the letters to the editor section in two primary ways. First, they encourage constituents and friends to write letters showing support for their work and policies. Most political campaigns compose sample letters in praise of the candidate that they provide for supporters to revise and submit to local papers. Second, politicians themselves may write letters to the editor responding to a newspaper article with which they disagree.

MEDIA INTERVIEWS

Those legislators with some rhetorical skills and ability to think on their feet usually agree to media interviews. Ranging from an appearance on a local call-in talk radio show to a magazine profile to a short series of on-camera questions from a national news anchor, interviews provide members of Congress opportunities to promote their positions and issues in their own words. Members and their communications staff weigh carefully each interview request, taking into consideration factors such as the medium (print, video, or audio), the nature of the interaction (one-on-one question and answer or a point-counterpoint format), and the perspective of the journalist. Legislators interested in seeking higher office or party leadership positions often seek opportunities for media interviews to increase their visibility.

STAGED EVENTS

Perhaps the best tool for proactive media strategy is the staged event created to generate media coverage. Historian Daniel Boorstin first described such media spectacles in 1961, coining the phrase **"pseudo-event"** to describe this "synthetic novelty which has flooded our experience"[18] that is characterized, in large part, by advance planning and the design to attract media attention. Such staged events can serve the needs of both politicians and journalists. Politicians want to call attention to their work, and many reporters appreciate a prepackaged story complete with camera-ready visuals and good sound bites.

Members of Congress plan several kinds of events that they hope will attract media attention. One example is the **press conference**, a targeted event designed to provide journalists an easy news story and allow them to ask questions. At such an event, a legislator might deliver a short speech promoting a policy idea, share the podium with celebrities or local activists who offer their support, and then entertain a few questions from reporters. At another common type of event, the **site visit**, legislators invite the press to join them as they tour a local business, community center, or school. In such a setting, the elected official can interact with constituents in their workplace while also creating an event that the media can report easily.

ANATOMY OF A PRESS CONFERENCE

To build interest in and support for Hart's legislation, her staff team began planning two major media events—one in the district and one in Washington. Hart wanted to include her local constituents in the process of introducing her safe-havens bill, so she decided to announce her legislative plans at a press conference in the Pittsburgh area. She hoped the event would educate the public and draw attention to the abandoned-infants problem. Brendan Benner, the press secretary, assembled a staff team to prepare everything the office would need to publicize the event.

Although the specific structure and schedule of press conferences can vary, most include several common elements. In particular, press secretaries like to make several resources available to journalists before and during the event to simplify their work and encourage positive press coverage.

MEDIA ADVISORIES

When possible, communications staff like to give journalists advance notice of events to encourage their attendance. A common way to invite the press is sending a **media advisory**. Similar in structure to a press release, the advisory alerts the news media to an upcoming event and includes essential information such as the date, time, and location. Although they cannot anticipate breaking news stories that might command their full attention on a given news day, reporters can reference media advisories to make tentative advance plans for covering stories. Many communications professionals follow up written media advisories with phone calls to reporters that encourage their participation and build interest in the event.

PRESS RELEASE

The night before and/or the day of the news conference, press secretaries send a press release to every print and broadcast media outlet that might cover the story. The release serves as a reminder to reporters already planning to attend, persuades others to add the event to their schedule, and provides media-ready content for those reporters who will not be present but might be prodded to write a story anyway.

PRESS KITS

Politicians may also assemble **press kits**, packets of information distributed to the journalists attending the event. Contents might include another copy of the press release, clippings of related news articles, a transcript of remarks prepared for the event, or biographies of participants in the press conference. Aides hope that reporters will reference the materials as they write stories about the event.

For Hart's initial press conference announcing the Safe Havens Support Act, her staff assembled press kits with materials tucked inside slick navy folders printed with the seal of the House of Representatives. Each folder contained a copy of the news release distributed in advance to journalists, an information sheet with answers to frequently asked questions, a sample "dear colleague" letter from Hart and Tubbs Jones, and a list of the bipartisan cosponsors of the bill. Figure 7.2 shows the information sheet inserted in each packet. The folder also included a clipping from *Woman's Day* magazine about babies abandoned at birth who are now thriving in their adoptive homes, a transcript of a National Public Radio broadcast about the need for publicity to raise awareness of safe havens programs, and a clipping from the *Beaver County Times* about a newborn baby found dead in a toilet in her mother's home.

FIGURE 7.2: SAFE HAVENS MEDIA INFORMATION SHEET

GENERAL QUESTIONS ABOUT BABY ABANDONMENT

How prevalent is newborn abandonment in the United States?

Unfortunately, no one has a definitive answer to this question. The federal government and most states do not keep statistics specific to abandoned newborns, and there is presently no way to determine what portion of infant homicides are due to abandonment.

- According to the Illinois Department of Children and Family Services, thirty-two to thirty-four infants were found abandoned each year from 1997 to 1999. Of these, approximately twenty infants are abandoned in the first twenty-four hours of their life.

- In the twelve months before Texas passed safe-havens legislation, thirty-three babies were discovered abandoned.

- According to a CNN review of FBI statistics, nearly five infants under the age of one are killed in the United States each week.

What is known about the abandoned babies and their birth parents?

To date, no research has been conducted to identify the population of parents who abandon their babies. The only information available is

continued

based on the few cases when authorities identify the parent, but such anecdotal data are not sufficient to draw definitive conclusions.

QUESTIONS ABOUT THE SAFE HAVENS SUPPORT ACT

How much will this cost the taxpayer?

This legislation requires no additional commitment of tax dollars. How much each state will devote to supporting infant abandonment programs will likely vary, but even a small amount of money can go a long way to informing the public about these programs.

Will this bill take money away from cash assistance and other TANF programs?

Most states have surpluses in their TANF block grants; that is, they are looking for productive uses for this money. No state is required to use TANF funds to support baby abandonment programs, but this bill does give them the flexibility to do so if they want.

When would this law take effect?

The law would be in effect the day the president signs the bill.

What about states that have not yet passed safe-havens bills?

Many states have safe-havens programs but do not yet have an infant abandonment law. A good example is our state—although Pennsylvania has yet to pass a safe-havens bill, A Hand to Hold is working here in Pittsburgh with the mayor and the district attorney to provide a safe place for abandoned babies. Even without a state law in place, states can use TANF funds to support programs like this one.

Source: Office of Congresswoman Melissa A. Hart (PA-04).

STAFF MEMBERS AVAILABLE TO REPORTERS

Perhaps more important than all the printed materials, staff members serve as a valuable resource for journalists attending a press conference. Once the formal speeches and questions end, reporters can interview aides to learn additional information and to ask for clarifications. Staff may choose to speak "on the record," providing direct quotes for media use, but they can also comment "off the record," adding details not for attribution. Such background information can give the reporter context for a story and offers a staff member more freedom to answer questions in detail.

CAPTURING LOCAL MEDIA COVERAGE: A SUCCESS STORY

Like most of her colleagues, Hart returns home to her district almost every weekend that Congress is in session. As soon as legislative business ends on Thursday night or Friday morning, she is on a plane back to Pittsburgh. Hart's scheduler knows the routine and thus books the congresswoman for events and meetings in the district between Friday and Monday. With this routine in mind, Hart and her staff selected Monday, June 25, as the date for her district press conference announcing Hart's plan to introduce the Safe Havens Support Act.

LOCATION, LOCATION

Several factors contribute to the choice of location for a media event. First, the ideal venue will have a symbolic value that connects naturally with the purpose of the meeting. Second, an ideal location will offer easy access for journalists and invited guests. Logistics, including readily available parking, a central location near offices of targeted media organizations, and sufficient signage, may improve the turnout. Even the choice of the specific room is important. An ideal room will offer plentiful space and electrical outlets for television camera operators, a sturdy podium with an appealing backdrop, and just enough chairs to seat everyone expected to attend.

After weighing these considerations, Hart and Benner decided to stage the event at the Children's Hospital of Pittsburgh. Since the purpose of the press conference was to draw attention to safe-havens programs that encouraged parents in crisis to relinquish unwanted newborns at hospitals or other designated locations, locating the event at a hospital was a natural fit. A recognized landmark with easy access for reporters and guests alike, Children's Hospital offered the assistance of an experienced media relations staff and office space equipped for hosting such events.

INVITED GUESTS

In addition to selecting a date and location, legislators and their aides must decide whom to invite to a press conference. Many criteria determine the invitation list. Because a primary goal is capturing as much media attention as possible, press secretaries look for high-profile participants whose celebrity alone may entice reporters to attend. Organizers also want to include other politicians and citizen activists who share concern for the cause.

Hart invited several local politicians to join her at the podium for the event. The district attorney of Lawrence County, Matthew Mangino, accepted the invitation. Mangino used this opportunity to announce that the three hospitals in his county had agreed to serve as designated safe havens for abandoned infants. Others participating included Patti Weaver, the Pittsburgh activist who first alerted Hart to the safe-havens issue, and Dr. Mary Clyde Pierce, the head of Children's Hospital's Child Advocacy Center.

RESULTING PRESS COVERAGE

Journalists from a variety of media outlets attended the Pittsburgh press conference. Two television stations sent camera crews, and several reporters attended. One reporter in attendance, Allison Schlesinger, worked for the Associated Press **wire service**. Newspapers purchase subscriptions to this service, which provides them access to news stories they can reprint in the paper. Knowing that Schlesinger's single story could appear in multiple papers, Hart's staff was thrilled that the Associated Press reporter covered the event.

Although planned weeks in advance, the press conference occurred one week after a newborn boy was found dead in Ellwood City, not far from Pittsburgh. The opportunity for reporters to hook Hart's legislative work with this tragic event likely heightened media attentiveness and raised the profile of the press conference.

The day after the event, articles appeared in the *Pittsburgh Post-Gazette* and on the front page of the *Beaver County Times*. Both pieces tied Hart's announcement with the story of the abandoned baby. The *Post-Gazette* article made the connection from the outset, beginning, "Efforts to promote 'safe havens' for unwanted infants got renewed attention yesterday in the wake of another tragic discovery: Police acting on an anonymous tip found a dead newborn wrapped in a towel in a wooded area of Ellwood City earlier this month."[19] After this introduction, the story quickly turned to the press conference, describing Hart's proposed legislation and quoting every person who spoke at the event. The *Beaver County Times* printed the Associated Press report. Beginning with Hart's proposal, the story then recounted the Ellwood City tragedy before quoting Hart and describing the goals of the Safe Havens Support Act.[20] The next day, the *Valley News Dispatch* endorsed Hart's bill in an editorial titled "'Safe Haven' Program Protects Newborns."[21]

Neither Hart nor her staff could control the news coverage of the press conference, but they were pleased with the results. Multiple outlets carried the story, and the accounts shed a positive light on the issue. From our perspective, the local press conference was a success.

STAGING A WASHINGTON PRESS CONFERENCE: PITFALLS AND SETBACKS

Buoyed by the positive results of the Pittsburgh media event, Hart and her staff next turned their attention to planning a press conference in Washington, D.C., that would showcase the bill and its sponsors. With so many members and senators competing for press coverage each day Congress is in session, we wanted to design an event that would draw media attention. The best way to increase interest is to include a high-profile participant, so the staff began brainstorming ideas of celebrities who might share a concern about the abandoned-infants tragedy.

In the early stages of planning, we pursued several possible guests. The first choice was talk show host Oprah Winfrey. We had several reasons for inviting the popular star. First and foremost, her celebrity would all but guarantee wide news coverage of the event. In addition, the safe-havens issue appeared to be a natural fit. The previous year, the *Oprah Winfrey Show* had devoted an hour-long program to the tragedy of abandoned infants and highlighted the work of safe-havens organizations. Finally, Hart was assisting a team at Winfrey's Web site, oxygen.com, contributing short articles describing her experiences as a first-year congresswoman. Hart's contacts at oxygen.com helped her connect directly with Winfrey's executive assistant and extend an official invitation to the press conference. In the end, Winfrey declined the request, saying she would be on vacation. Using connections with media-savvy outside groups, we extended invitations to other celebrities. None accepted, but we continued planning the Washington press conference all the same.

As the likelihood of a celebrity guest faded, the press secretary decided to set a date for the event and move forward. He consulted with Tubbs Jones's office; scheduled the press conference for Tuesday, July 31; and began the early preparations. Other staff continued the search for the right guests to invite, shifting their focus from celebrities to safe-havens activists. John M. Tyson Jr., the district attorney from Mobile, Alabama, who worked with Jodi Brooks to create the first infant safe-havens program, agreed to join the congresswomen to discuss the issue. The plans were finally coming together.

A few weeks before the planned news conference, the television newsmagazine *Dateline NBC* ran a segment titled "Secret Baby." The program told the story of Kellie Moye and her parents, Jim and Sue. On February 11, 1996, a resident living next door to the Moye family in Poplar Grove, Illinois, discovered the body of a dead baby girl in a snowbank near their back door. Horrified by this tragic discovery, concerned townsfolk named the infant Angelica Faith and arranged a funeral and burial. A police investigation into the death yielded no leads. Kellie Moye, a high school student when the baby was found, had since graduated and moved in with her on-again, off-again boyfriend, Michael Mirshak. After the two argued one evening, Kellie called her parents for help. On their way to help Kellie, Jim and Sue saw Michael and confronted him. In the ensuing conversation, Michael revealed a secret that he and Kellie had been hiding for almost five years: Kellie was the mother of the abandoned baby, Angelica Faith. When the Moyes asked their daughter about this, she confirmed Michael's story, tearfully explaining that she thought the neighbors would find the baby and never wanted her child to die. The Moyes called a friend on the police force and told him their story. Kellie was charged with the murder, found guilty of a lesser charge of involuntary manslaughter, and sentenced to a four-year prison term. Wanting to spare other families their heartbreak and hoping to encourage scared pregnant women to seek alternatives to abandoning a baby unsafely, Kellie and her parents shared their experiences with *Dateline*.[22]

Stirred by the Moyes' willingness to share their tragedy to help others, Hart's staff invited them to Washington to tell their story at the Safe Havens Support Act press conference. A private couple who preferred to avoid the media spotlight, the Moyes weighed the invitation for a few days, finally agreeing to travel to Washington. They were willing to discuss their family's tragedy again because they believed it could save lives. Abandoned-infants activist Dawn Geras (first introduced in chapter 4) and her husband Bob agreed to accompany the Moyes on the trip.

A flurry of planning followed. Almost every staff member in Hart's office worked on the preparations in anticipation of the congresswoman hosting her first national press conference. Wanting to make the most of the guests' time on Capitol Hill, we began scheduling meetings so that the five activists could tell their stories to other members of Congress and enlist their support for a safe-havens bill.

A few days before the event, Tubbs Jones's legislative director called Hart's office with some bad news. Congresswoman Tubbs Jones had a last-minute schedule change that would keep her in Cleveland into the following week. Hart should feel free to continue with the press conference as planned, but her primary Democratic cosponsor would not be able to attend.

TURNING LEMONS INTO LEMONADE:
SAFE HAVENS LOBBY DAY

When Hart learned the news of the schedule change, she canceled the press conference. She wanted to raise awareness of the Safe Havens Support Act, but she did not want to exclude Tubbs Jones.

The same day that Hart canceled the press conference, the scheduler for Speaker of the House Dennis Hastert called to say that the Speaker could meet with the Illinois and Alabama guests. Armed with this new information, I called Dawn Geras and John Tyson to tell them the bad news about the press conference but offered a counterproposal. The Speaker of the House wanted to meet with them. The plane and hotel arrangements had already been made, so why not turn the day in Washington into an opportunity to lobby important decision makers? Tyson said he would continue with his plans. After discussion with Jim and Sue Moye, Dawn Geras told us that the Illinois delegation would still come.

By the time the guests arrived in Washington, they had a full schedule of events awaiting them. Monday evening, they gathered with Congresswoman Hart, her chief of staff, and me for dinner and discussion. The next morning, Safe Havens Lobby Day began with a meeting with Sarah Gesiriech, the White House associate director of public policy, who handled adoption and child welfare issues for the president. The guests then traveled to Capitol Hill for meetings with five members of Congress.

The anticipated highlight of the day, the meeting with Speaker Hastert, was yet another victim to members' rapidly changing schedules. With the House of Representatives poised to adjourn for the August recess, work was moving at a frantic pace, and Hastert was trying to negotiate an agreement on a controversial reform. The Speaker sent his apologies with KiKi Kless, assistant to the Speaker for policy, who spent almost an hour listening to the Moyes share their story and learning about safe havens work in Alabama and Illinois. Although Hastert himself never appeared, Kless clearly communicated the Speaker's strong support for Hart's bill and his willingness to move the legislation quickly.

As the shift from press conference to lobby day demonstrates, events change quickly in the fast pace and flurry of congressional activity. Although Hart did not achieve her original goal of attracting national media attention to the abandoned-infants problem and her work toward a solution, she did succeed in raising the awareness of key policymakers. Pleased with the local press response to her efforts and armed with a commitment from the Speaker of the House to help move legislation forward, Hart was finally ready to introduce her safe-havens bill.

CHAPTER SUMMARY

In order to attract attention to their ideas and build support for their programs, members of Congress need to develop and implement media strategies. The news media are the primary source of political information for most Americans, so savvy legislators know they must work with national and local journalists to raise awareness of their issues and policies.

Members of Congress face many challenges as they seek media attention. Members compete with one another and with other political institutions for the few stories that might receive national news coverage in a given day. Legislators also compete for attention in the local press, building relationships with journalists at home in the hopes of reaching their constituents through local print and broadcast media.

After introducing some of the tools of the communications trade that press aides commonly use to capture public and media attention, this chapter examined Hart's media strategy for raising awareness of her safe-havens proposal. Focusing on two major events, one in the district and one in Washington, these practical examples describe one media success and one near failure and demonstrate the importance of flexibility in the high-speed, high-intensity environment of Congress.

Notes

1. Doris Graber, *Mass Media and American Politics*, 6th ed. (Washington, D.C.: Congressional Quarterly Press, 2002), 3.
2. David Price, *The Congressional Experience*, 3rd ed. (Boulder, Colo.: Westview Press, 2004), 245.
3. Vincent L. Hutchings, *Public Opinion and Democratic Accountability: How Citizens Learn about Politics* (Princeton, N.J.: Princeton University Press, 2003).
4. C. Danielle Vinson, *Local Media Coverage of Congress and Its Members: Through Local Eyes* (Cresskill, N.J.: Hampton Press, 2003), 169.
5. Ibid., 2.
6. Ibid., 97.
7. "Nielsen Media Research Local Universe Estimates" (accessed at http://www.nielsenmedia.com/DMAs.html).
8. *Pittsburgh Post-Gazette*, "About Us: Media Kit" (accessed at http://www.post-gazette.com/mediakit/14.asp).
9. The circulation number aggregates the estimated daily circulation of the two papers based on their internal reports. For more information, see "2005 Retail Advertising Rates" (accessed at http://www1800909trib.com/advertising/pghtrib_retailrates2005.pdf and http://www.1800909trib.com/advertising/GBGretailrates_05.pdf).
10. "Nielsen Media Research Local Universe Estimates."
11. Karen M. Kedrowski, *Media Entrepreneurs and the Media Enterprise in the U.S. Congress* (Cresskill, N.J.: Hampton Press, 1996), 16–17.
12. Ibid., 194.
13. Jason Salzman, *Making the News: A Guide for Activists and Nonprofits* (Boulder, Colo.: Westview Press, 2003), 162.
14. Debbie Wachter Morris, "Ellport Pair Held after Police Find Baby in Plastic Bag," *New Castle News*, June 18, 2001, A1.
15. For a complete listing of the winners of CongressOnline's Best Web Sites on Capitol Hill, see http://www.cmfweb.org/mouseawards2003.asp. Representative Hart's Web site can be accessed at http://www.house.gov/hart.
16. Vinson, 96.
17. For a more detailed discussion of the editorial leanings of various news outlets, see David Paletz, *The Media in American Politics*, 2nd ed. (New York: Longman, 2002), appendix A, "Commentary."
18. Daniel J. Boorstin, *The Image: A Guide to Pseudo-Events in America* (New York: Vintage Books, 1992), 9.
19. Sally Kalson, "Hart Pushes 'Safe Havens' for Unwanted Infants," *Pittsburgh Post-Gazette*, June 16, 2001, B3.
20. Allison Schlesinger, "Let's Offer Safe Haven for Babies, Hart Asks," *Beaver County Times*, 26 June, 2001, p. A-1.
21. "'Safe Haven' Program Protects Newborns," *Valley News Dispatch*, June 27, 2001.
22. *Dateline NBC*, "Secret Baby," July 9, 2001 (accessed at http://www.msnbc.com/news/596538.asp).

8

FINDING A WAY TO THE FLOOR

A BILL BECOMES TWO LAWS

Having secured support for the Safe Havens Support Act within the chamber and in the media, Representative Hart saw momentum quickly grow in favor of the bill. Armed with a growing bipartisan list of cosponsors and letters of support from a diverse set of public service organizations, trade associations, and other interest groups, Hart believed that the time was right to introduce her bill in the House.

From the beginning, Hart and her staff knew that a stand-alone bill would have little if any chance of reaching the House floor. Most of the thousands of bills introduced during each session are referred to committees and never see further congressional action. Congresswoman Hart, however, was not willing to introduce a bill, claim credit for her work to combat infant abandonment, and move on to other issues. Her goal from the outset was to find a way to ensure that this bill would become law. Although passing the bill on its own would be her preference, she knew that Congress would be most likely to address the issue of infant abandonment if safe-havens provisions were added as an amendment to another bill already working its way through the legislative process.

As discussed in chapter 5, Congress creates and funds many programs for a limited number of years. When programs near their expiration, Congress must pass legislation to renew them, or they will end. Hart thus reasoned that if she could convince the party leadership to incorporate all or part of her safe-havens proposal into a popular bill up for **reauthorization**, it could ride the coattails of another program and become law.

This chapter follows H.R. 2018 through the final stages of the legislative process from its official introduction on the floor of the House to its transformation into an amendment to a much larger child welfare law. After discussing the purpose of the committee process, the chapter considers the role of committee staff and how they assisted Hart's office with her bill. A final section describes the process of moving bills from committees through floor debate all the way to the president's desk for signature into law.

INTO THE HOPPER: INTRODUCING LEGISLATION

Although anyone can try to persuade them to act, only legislators themselves have the authority to introduce a bill. The formal process of introducing legislation includes several steps. First, the sponsor must prepare a draft in a set form and style; staff at the Office of Legislative Counsel typically provide this service. In the House of Representatives, members or delegates place a signed copy of their bill in the "**hopper**," a box located next to the rostrum at the front of the chamber. Senators either give a copy of their bill to the clerk or request recognition from the presiding officer and formally introduce their legislation in a speech. The clerks in each chamber assign each bill a unique identifying number. Public bills in the House begin with "H.R." to denote the House of Representatives, Senate bill numbers begin with an "S." Typically, the majority party reserves a few numbers (often one through ten) for major legislative initiatives, and numbering begins sequentially with each subsequent bill introduced throughout the two-year Congress. The Safe Havens Support Act, for example, was assigned the number H.R. 2018, identifying it as the 2,018th bill introduced in the House during the 107th Congress.

Once received in its chamber, a bill is assigned to one or more committees for consideration. The presiding officers of each chamber have the official authority to make committee assignments, but in general practice the parliamentarian reads incoming bills and decides on referrals. H.R. 2018 was referred to two committees: Education and Workforce and Ways and Means.

After its official introduction, the legislation debuts in the next issue of the *Congressional Record*. A copy also goes to the government printing office so that the text will be accessible to other members and the general public.

THE COMMITTEE PROCESS

Congress could not function in the modern era without the committee process. As the federal government has expanded in size and scope, so have the demands on members of Congress increased dramatically. Legislators write and renew bills affecting almost every possible issue, and they share with the president oversight of the vast federal bureaucracy that includes the fifteen cabinet-level departments as well as numerous independent regulatory commissions, government corporations, and independent agencies. Committees and their staff provide the institutional means and expertise to manage this vast workload facing Congress.[1]

Committees serve both institutional and individual purposes. Institutionally, they are the centers of policymaking, governmental oversight, and public education. As two congressional scholars summarize, committees are the "means by which Congress sifts through an otherwise impossible jumble of bills, proposals, and issues."[2] With 435 members, the House of Representatives is the largest legislative body in the world; this group assembled cannot evaluate everything brought before it. The process is almost equally daunting in the smaller 100-member Senate, which still cannot even begin to process the thousands of bills introduced each session. Thus, the House and the Senate developed committee systems to divide labor and distribute the workload. By sending proposed bills to committees for consideration, smaller groups of legislators can work simultaneously on a variety of issues and concerns as representatives of the entire chamber.

Likewise, committees have an individual role, serving the needs of members in important ways. One classic formulation of committee work in Congress outlines three basic goals of legislators: reelection, influence within the chamber, and making good public policy.[3] Committee work allows members to pursue each of these goals. First, committee service can help with reelection. Assignment to high-profile committees increases legislators' visibility and enhances their name recognition. Membership on committees with jurisdiction over issues of particular importance to one's district or state is also valuable at the ballot box. Second, members gain power and influence through their length of service on and the relative prestige of their committees. Committee chairs, usually among the longer-serving members of the panel, have great authority within the chamber because of their gatekeeper role. Third, because they are divided by subject-matter jurisdiction, committees also offer their members a place to develop public policy expertise. A member of the Armed Services Committee, for instance, can become knowledgeable regarding military and defense policy, developing proficiency to discuss these issues in the media and with constituents.

TYPES OF COMMITTEES

Congress divides its work between three types of committees. **Standing committees**—permanent committees with fixed subject-matter jurisdictions—receive proposals for legislation and process them into bills. Labor is further divided between **subcommittees** that have more specific jurisdictions and report to the parent committee. Ranging from the Judiciary to International Relations to Small Business, the House has twenty standing committees with eighty-four subcommittees. The Senate divides its work between sixteen committees and sixty-eight subcommittees.

A second category, **select committees**, includes temporary committees that primarily hold hearings and highlight issues. Typically, these panels do not have the power to report legislation to the chamber for a vote. A few select committees, such as those on Ethics and Intelligence, continue from Congress to Congress. In general practice, however, most select committees form for a stated purpose and disband when they complete their appointed task. Examples include the committees that investigated Watergate and Iran-Contra.

Joint committees include representatives from both the House and the Senate. Permanent joint committees have equal representation from both chambers and rotate the chair position between the House and the Senate every two years. Small panels that receive little public attention, four such committees have permanent status: Economic, Library, Printing, and Taxation. A special form of joint committee, a **conference committee**, convenes temporarily to reach a compromise on legislation passed in different forms by the House and Senate.

THE COMMITTEE ASSIGNMENT PROCESS

At the beginning of each new Congress, party leaders determine the size and the ratio of Democrats to Republicans on each committee. The partisan balance on the committees is supposed to reflect the balance in the chamber; thus, the majority party always has leadership control of each committee. Once the leaders agree on these numbers, they ask legislators to state their preference of committee assignments. Most incumbents ask to retain their committees from the previous Congress, whereas newly elected members or those seeking positions on the most coveted panels will list an order of preferences. In general, members usually get assignments that they want, but the party leadership has the final authority and resolves any disputes. Each party caucus has its own panel to allocate positions: the names vary from the steering committee in the House to the committee on committees for Senate Republicans and the steering and coordination committee for Senate Democrats.

Because the party controls committee assignments, the process can be a tool for party discipline. In the 107th Congress, for example, rogue Ohio Democrat James Traficant publicly expressed his dissatisfaction with his party leaders by voting for Republican Dennis Hastert for Speaker of the House. The party responded by denying him any committee assignments.

House leadership categorizes committees in three ways: exclusive, nonexclusive, or exempt. As a general rule, members assigned to the exclusive committees (Appropriations, Energy and Commerce, Rules, and Ways and Means) serve on only that panel. Members may serve on more than one of the nonexclusive committees; most serve on two or three. Very few legislators request the low-profile exempt committees such as Library or Post Office, so they do not count toward overall limits on committee service.

The assignment process is more rigid in the Senate. Each committee is assigned a letter: A (senators serve on no more than two), B (senators can serve on only one), and C (senators may serve on as many as they would like). In recent years, the Senate has added an additional category, a subset of the A committees known as "Super A." Since this designation consists of the most prestigious committees—Appropriations, Armed Services, Finance, and Foreign Relations—senators can have only one Super A assignment.

After the respective committees on committees meet and decide on assignments, each submits its slate to the party conference for a vote. Once the party votes are complete, each chamber votes on acceptance of the Republican and Democratic lists. In most cases, these votes simply ratify party decisions.

COMMITTEE LEADERSHIP

Each committee is led by a chair, the member of the majority party selected to oversee the committee's work. By choosing what bills to consider, scheduling meetings, and presiding over committee business, the **committee chair** exerts great control over the legislative process. The member of the minority party with the longest continuous service on the panel, known as the **ranking member**, acts as spokesperson and provides leadership for fellow partisans.

The selection of committee leaders varies in the two chambers. The hierarchy within each committee was traditionally determined by seniority: the member of the majority party with the longest committee service automatically became the chair. Since the reforms in the 1970s, however, chairs have been elected by a majority vote of the party conference, overriding the seniority system and giving party power brokers more influence on members' actions. House Republicans changed the process even more dramatically when they gained control of the chamber in the 104th Congress and implemented term limits on committee chairs. Speaker Dennis Hastert added further reforms, requiring all prospective chairs to submit to an interview process in which they present party leaders a proposal for how they would organize the committee and outline their legislative agenda, oversight plan, and communications strategy. In the Senate, Republican committee chairs have six-year term limits, but otherwise the seniority system generally dominates the process.

COMMITTEE REFERRALS

The parliamentarian in each chamber determines where to refer bills when they are introduced. Because some legislative proposals are complex and cover multiple substantive policy issues and the jurisdiction of standing committees can overlap, the decision of where to refer a newly introduced bill is not a simple one. In complex cases, a bill may receive multiple referrals; that is, sections of a bill are sent to different committees for review and consideration. The failed attempt at comprehensive health care reform presented early in the Clinton administration, for instance, had overlapping jurisdiction among five House and Senate committees. Because, as one observer described, "each and every one of those [committees] expected to have a 'piece of the action,'" power politics exacerbated by multiple referrals impeded passage of the bill.[4]

Because of the volume of bills introduced each Congress, committees do not have enough time or interest to consider every bill sent to them. For this reason, most bills introduced in Congress "die in committee." A committee chair thus exercises great power by crafting the panel's agenda. Bills of great importance for the chair, the majority party, or (in many cases) majority members of the committee are most likely to receive consideration. In contrast, bills sponsored by the minority party or policies that are unpopular with party leaders rarely see further congressional action.

Members and senators often craft legislation with specific language designed to direct the referral, seeking to maximize the likelihood that their bills will be referred to committees on which they serve. When discussing the working draft of the Safe Havens Support Act, for example, the attorney from Legislative Counsel drafting Hart's bill asked what department of the federal government should have oversight over the legislation. Health and Human Services was the most natural department for studying the abandoned-infants issue and managing money to help states with safe-havens programs, but the attorney asked whether we might prefer to give jurisdiction to the Justice Department. After all, safe-havens laws remove or reduce criminal penalties. Because, he pointed out, Hart was a member of the judiciary committee, she would find it easier to influence the direction of the bill if it went there. In the end, however, the congresswoman decided not to divert the policy to the Justice Department since Health and Human Services includes the policy experts most aware of and likely best able to understand and address the issues related to infant abandonment.

ROLES AND FUNCTIONS OF COMMITTEE STAFF

In order to process the hundreds of bills referred to committees each congressional term, the chambers provide staff to assist the chair and ranking member with their work. The **majority staff** work for the committee chair and typically have more resources and office space than the **minority staff**, a separate office of professionals who work on behalf of the committee members from the minority party. Any time that party control changes in the House or Senate, the control of the committees and their staff offices will reverse.

Similar to the chief of staff in a representative or senator's personal office, the **staff director** runs a committee office and reports to the chair or ranking member. Offices also include a team of policy experts, typically called **professional staff**. Many committees also hire lawyers, called **counsel**, one of whom usually sits with the chair and the ranking member during meetings to provide advice on parliamentary procedure. Legal counsel also assist with writing and amending legislation and provide legal advice. Many committee offices also include communications staff who craft media talking points, prepare members for markups, and court media attention.

Together, the staff on each committee serve as a bridge between members and legislative programs, offering advice for leaders and individual legislators alike. In particular, they provide an important source of institutional knowledge for Congress. Because committee staff devote all of their time to a narrowly defined groups of issues, they truly become experts. Staff members understand the practical aspects of complex policies, develop contacts with experts in state and national government, and learn the rhythms of the institution and its leaders. If a member is looking for a way to navigate through the legislative process, committee staff provide valuable insights and practical political advice.

WORKING WITH COMMITTEES ON SAFE HAVENS: FINDING THE RIGHT VEHICLE

Hart was able to build strong bipartisan support for the Safe Havens Support Act for several reasons. The subject matter—assisting states trying to save lives of newborn babies—was laudable and relatively uncontroversial. In addition, the design of funding the bill through an already existing program so as to require no new government spending appealed to fiscal conservatives.

Finding an existing bill that could enfold the Safe Havens Support Act would not be a simple task. Our knowledge of existing programs was limited; we needed to work with other congressional staff who had more specialized expertise. With this in mind, we decided to approach committee staff for their assistance. H.R. 2018 had been referred to two committees: Ways and Means and Education and Workforce. Ways and Means had jurisdiction over most child welfare bills, so we met with them first.

Legislative Counsel Bill Rys and I scheduled a meeting with Matt Weidinger, the staff director of the Human Resources Subcommittee of Ways and Means, to discuss safe havens and get ideas for how to push the bill forward. Weidinger and his staff indicated their willingness to work with us, but they did not like the funding mechanism in Hart's bill. He explained their serious concerns about the bill's provision to fund safe havens by amending Temporary Assistance for Needy Families (TANF). What Hart thought was a creative way to fund safe havens without adding to federal spending (as discussed in chapter 5) made committee staff unwilling to support attaching H.R. 2018 to another bill. TANF, the program created by the welfare reform efforts in the mid-1990s, was an immense government program with at least as many detractors as supporters. The committee staff expected TANF reauthorization to be a divisive partisan battle. Therefore, they were not pleased with the suggestion of adding yet another piece to the existing program, nor did they want Hart's bill highlighting the surplus TANF funds available in many states. We needed the committee's assistance to improve the chance of the bill moving forward and wanted to keep the debate over safe havens as far from controversy as possible. Once Hart saw the political wisdom of avoiding TANF, she was willing to find another, better (it was hoped) means of ensuring that some version of the safe-havens bill would become a law.

Through conversations with committee staff and the Congressional Research Service, the office identified several federal programs that address subjects related to infant safe havens. We considered the strengths and weaknesses of the various programs as we searched for the program that would best fit with Hart's goals.

ABANDONED INFANTS ASSISTANCE ACT

Initially, the Abandoned Infants Assistance Act (AIA) seemed a perfect fit for H.R. 2018. We soon learned, however, that this program addressed a different category of abandoned infants than those safe havens sought to save. Originally created during the initial AIDS crisis, the AIA provides demonstration grants for organizations and facilities that offer services for "boarder babies," infants abandoned in hospitals after the mother gives birth. The program gives preference to HIV-infected and drug-addicted infants, the babies most likely to be left behind because of their special needs. Although the program was due for reauthorization, committee staff noted that no one was looking to either expand or contract the program.

At least from its title, the AIA sounded like it would be a good fit for incorporating safe-havens programs, and the scheduled reauthorization was good timing. But the disadvantages to this bill far outweighed any perceived benefits. The AIA was a very small program (authorizing $13 million in grants) with no call for expansion. It would need significant funding increases to address the needs of an additional category of abandoned babies, those infants discarded and left to die. Any program considered for reauthorization has a constituency who currently benefits from the funding and wants to protect what they currently receive. As we quickly learned when investigating the AIA, those who provide services funded by this program describe the issue of babies abandoned in public places as insignificant when compared with the number of boarder babies. If Hart tried to incorporate her bill into this existing program, she would be entering a "turf battle" that could get divisive.

PROMOTING SAFE AND STABLE FAMILIES

Matt Weidinger suggested that safe-havens programs might be a better fit with the Promoting Safe and Stable Families (PSSF) program, which was scheduled for reauthorization in September 2001. Subpart 2 of Title IV-B of the Social Security Act, PSSF was designed to direct child welfare dollars for new, more innovative services and to provide a vehicle for Congress to target these funds more directly. PSSF money is distributed as a formula grant to states based on the percentages of children in each state eligible for food stamps, a measure designed to distribute the money in rough proportion to the number of children living in poverty. State child welfare agencies allocate the money at their discretion according to the principles outlined in the act. The existing PSSF program provided $305 million to be used in four general categories: family preservation services, family support services, time-limited family reunification services, and adoption promotion and support. The Department of Health and Human Services guidelines directed states to spend at least 20 percent of the monies in each of the four categories, but at that time states were spending the most (40 percent) for family support and the least (15 percent) for adoption promotion and support, the category that was the natural fit for safe-havens promotion.

Weighing advantages and disadvantages of trying to incorporate safe havens into this program suggested many strong reasons to consider this route. First, S. 685, a bill sponsored by Senator Evan Bayh (D-Ind.), was already moving through the 107th Congress to reauthorize the program at $505 million. President Bush also signaled his support for PSSF, requesting a budget increase for this program of $200 million, about a 75 percent increase. According to committee staff, no other child welfare bill would likely see a funding increase anytime soon. The bill also seemed a good fit because the goal of PSSF, targeting children and families at risk, was very much in line with the purpose of the Safe Havens Support Act. A conversation with an expert from the Congressional Research Service suggested that this program had stronger political support on Capitol Hill than many other child welfare programs because of the states' ability to direct the dollars where they saw fit.

Although the program had many selling points, there were also some disadvantages to linking safe havens with PSSF. States and localities receiving this funding must match 25 percent of the federal grants with their own monies. Additionally, committee staff noted that they were feeling pressure to change the distribution of funds so as to provide more money for family support services and less for adoption promotion and support, potentially moving money away from the services that could support safe-havens programs.

OTHER POTENTIAL REVENUE SOURCES

Committee staff discussed a few other child welfare programs that might also be good matches for safe-havens programs. Although Safe and Stable Families seemed the most natural choice, we hoped to find as many options for potential legislative vehicles as possible.

After reviewing several programs, we found a bill that we thought might also work well with safe-havens proposals, the Child Abuse Prevention and Treatment Act (CAPTA), and the Community-Based Family Resource and Support Grants created as part of this legislation. Overlapping somewhat with PSSF, the family resource grants provide funds to community-based organizations instead of state governments, directing the money to programs for at-risk families.

Like many other child welfare programs, the purpose of these grants fit well with safe-havens programs. The timing and political mood was also promising, as CAPTA was a popular program that was expected to succeed with reauthorization that fall. Unlike the other child welfare programs we were considering, CAPTA was under the jurisdiction of the Education and Workforce Committee, not Ways and Means. To make progress including safe havens in the CAPTA reauthorization, we would need to work with another group of committee staff members. Experts at the Congressional Research Service warned us that these grants serve very vested interests; the organizations that receive these funds are very protective of their dollars.

Having identified two programs to target, Hart sought ways to work with the committees considering both PSSF and CAPTA to maximize the opportunities for adding safe havens to either or both bills.

COMMITTEE PROCEDURE

After legislation is referred to committee, most chairs delegate work even further, referring each proposal to a **subcommittee** for initial action on a bill. Whether in full committee or in one of its subcommittees, committee consideration of a bill follows a three-step process.

PUBLIC HEARINGS

First, the chair decides if a bill will be the subject of a **public hearing**: an open session for discussion of a proposal and its possible implications. Committee staff (often in coordination with a bill's sponsor) invite experts to testify. Common witnesses include a bill's sponsor, federal officials with jurisdiction over proposed programs, and representatives from organized interests that have a stake in the outcome. Private citizens may also testify at a hearing; a bill's supporters often look for celebrities to add media interest to a hearing or invite constituents to share their relevant experiences. The panel of experts usually includes witnesses invited in consultation with the majority and minority committee staff, but the panel will include more participants testifying in favor of the legislation than detractors.

Most hearings follow a similar format. After the chair and ranking member offer opening remarks, the participants usually read prepared statements and then answer questions from committee members.

Although designed as opportunities to inform members and the public about pending legislation, hearings are more likely tools for publicity than for deliberative discussion. Committee members may use their question time to praise a popular figure or make a political point on the record, just as sponsors may reward friendly collaborators with the opportunity to testify before Congress.

Hart's office worked with the Education and Workforce Committee to plan a hearing on reauthorization of CAPTA. Committee Chairman John Boehner referred the bill to the subcommittee on select education; the subcommittee decided to hold two hearings. The first hearing, held on August 2, 2001, included testimony evaluating the strengths and weaknesses of the CAPTA program up for reauthorization.[5]

With encouragement from Hart and others, the subcommittee staff convened a second hearing to discuss child welfare issues not covered under current law. The panel of witnesses included Patti Weaver, the Pittsburgh activist who first brought the safe-havens issue to Hart's attention. Weaver testified about her work as the founder and president of A Hand to Hold, the purposes of infant safe-havens programs, and estimates of how many lives such programs save each year. Arguing for increased funding of these programs, Weaver explained, "Better funding to safe haven programs would enable them to get out the word faster, reach more people, and ultimately save lives. Funding these organizations will ensure that we have a safety net for the approximately 1,000 babies a year that might die from abandonment."[6] Working with the committee staff, Hart was able to bring national attention to the infant abandonment problem and showcase the work of a former constituent.

COMMITTEE MARKUPS

The next stage of the committee process is the **markup**. In these sessions, committee members review the proposed text of a bill and decide on the final language. In some instances, the committee accepts the original text in very swift action. For more complex or controversial legislation, however, a markup can be very contentious. If a chair would like to make changes to a proposal, a markup will begin with the chair offering what is called the **chairman's mark amendment** for the first vote. If passed, the chair's version of the bill becomes the text under consideration for the remainder of the session. Committee members can offer revisions in one of two forms: an amendment, a proposal that changes some of the wording, or an amendment in the nature of a substitute, a proposal that replaces the original bill with something different. After discussion, the committee votes to accept or reject each amendment or substitute. Once all amendments have been considered, the committee holds a final vote to determine if they should forward the bill to the chamber for possible consideration. If a majority agrees, the bill is then reported out of the committee.

When looking for help enfolding the Safe Havens Support Act into another bill, Matt Weidinger and others from the Ways and Means Subcommittee on Human Resources encouraged Hart to work with a committee member from her state to amend the Safe and Stable Families Act. As Weidinger explained, if Hart could not convince this person to support her bill, the legislation had no real hope of success. The congresswoman found the assistance she needed from another Pennsylvanian, Phil English. Before winning his seat in the House, English had worked in Hart's state senate office as her chief of staff; the two members and their staffs had a good working relationship. English liked Hart's proposal and agreed to offer an amendment during the subcommittee markup. On September 25, 2001, English proposed a change that gave states permission to use Safe and Stable Families money to promote safe-havens programs. The amendment passed by voice vote, thus enfolding most of HR 2018 into the larger bill.

COMMITTEE REPORTS

Bills that successfully pass a markup session reach the final step of the committee process: reporting. With the help of their staff, committee chairs report a bill out of committee, providing the chamber with the final wording of the bill determined in the markup. Committees often include formal written reports to accompany complex bills. Written from the majority's perspective, **committee reports** may include transcripts of the committee sessions, recorded votes, and explanations and description of actions taken. Members of the committee who disagree with the narrative can append their additional or dissenting views, a matter of great importance given the political implications of committee reports. Because they document committee actions and offer reasons for decisions made in the process, reports provide a record that members of the executive branch and federal judges can use to interpret congressional intent.

By the time a bill is reported out of committee, the language of a bill may have changed dramatically. However similar to or different than the wording and content the sponsor first introduced, the committee version is the final one that is recommended to the House or Senate for consideration.

FROM THE COMMITTEE TO THE FLOOR

If a committee reports a bill favorably, it joins other proposals waiting for possible consideration by the chamber. The House and Senate have different processes to manage the flow of bills.[7]

HOUSE CALENDARS

Given the size of the House of Representatives, much of the legislative business occurs when the chamber resolves into the **Committee of the Whole**, the forum in which members debate and amend legislation under a different set of rules that expedite their work. Under House rules, all bills that include taxes or spending must be considered by the Committee of the Whole.

A bill reported from a House committee is usually placed on one of two calendars to wait for further legislative action. Most public bills go to the **union calendar** and are numbered in the order received; those bills that, by House rules, do not demand consideration by the Committee of the Whole are placed on the **house calendar**.

The rules of the House provide for three other calendars: all private bills, those that apply only to specific individuals, go on the **private calendar** and may be brought to the floor for consideration on the first or third Tuesday of each month. The **corrections calendar** includes noncontroversial bills that are intended to make minor corrections to federal rules, regulations, and court decisions. The House can consider these bills on the second and fourth Tuesdays of each month, but passage requires a favorable vote by at least a three-fifths majority. Formal proposals to force movement of bills "stuck" in committee, if they garner support from a majority of the chamber's members, go to the **calendar of motions to discharge committees**.

THE SENATE LEGISLATIVE CALENDAR

Legislative proposals referred from Senate committees go to the general orders section of the **Senate legislative calendar**. Numbered in the order they are received, all bills eligible for floor consideration wait on this calendar. The Senate has constitutional authority to offer advice and consent on several presidential actions; once reported out of committee, these measures are placed on the **executive calendar**, which is divided into sections for pending nominations, resolutions, and treaties.

FROM CALENDAR TO FLOOR BUSINESS

Most of the work in the House of Representatives is governed by **special resolutions**, commonly called "**rules**." Rules provide restrictions to limit debate and manage floor activity. When a committee chair reports a bill favorably, the chair can place a bill on one of the House calendars or can send it to the Rules Committee. The **Rules Committee** writes resolutions for special consideration that may include provisions for the length of debate on a bill, the number of amendments allowed (if any), and the order of consideration of amendments. By sending a special resolution to the floor, the committee provides a way for the chamber to consider a bill immediately. Most bills reach the House floor through the Rules Committee, giving this panel great power and influence over the legislative process.

Bills can also reach the House floor through other provisions. If all members agree by unanimous consent, a measure can be brought up for debate. A more common mechanism, a **motion to suspend the rules**, allows the House to consider uncontroversial bills with relative speed. On Mondays and Tuesdays as well as the last six days of each session, the Speaker can entertain this motion and bring bills to the floor. Debate on bills considered under suspension is limited to forty minutes; to pass, a bill must receive at least a two-thirds vote, not the simple majority required under the regular rules.

The Senate, the more deliberative of the two chambers, operates with less rigidity and efficiency. One prevailing tradition, **unlimited debate**, recognizes the right of each senator to speak on the floor without limitation. Another norm, **unanimous consent**, requires everyone present to agree before an action can commence. Taken together, these two provisions give individual senators significant power over legislative activity.

In order to move legislation through the chamber expeditiously, senators work behind the scenes to craft **unanimous consent agreements** (or UCAs), provisions that work similar to rules in the House by limiting debate and setting parameters on amendments. Although UCAs do require that every senator present vote for the measure, such an agreement rarely reaches the floor for a vote unless bipartisan negotiations indicate it will receive unanimous consent.

FROM CHAMBER TO CHAMBER

The Constitution requires that the House and Senate pass bills in identical form. To accomplish this goal, proposals may move through the two chambers in several different ways. The traditional path for legislation begins in one chamber and works its way to the floor for a vote. On passage, the bill then moves to the other chamber for consideration there. Because the process of working through each chamber is so lengthy, senators and representatives often introduce high-profile legislation as "**companion bills**," identical or similar proposals that work their way through the House and Senate simultaneously.

Whatever path is chosen, the wording of all but the simplest resolutions is likely to change during the legislative process. For those instances when a bill passes the House and the Senate in different forms, the two chambers must reconcile these differences. Sometimes, one chamber will accept the other's work and vote on the bill as it passed in the other chamber. When such agreement is impossible, the Speaker and the majority leaders in the Senate can appoint a **conference committee** for negotiating changes acceptable to both chambers. Usually comprised of members of the House and Senate committees that considered the bill in question, such a temporary panel meets as needed to seek common ground. If the conference committee cannot reach agreement, the legislation fails. If they reach an acceptable compromise, they produce a **conference report** that includes new wording of the bill for each chamber to consider in a simple up-or-down vote. If the bill reported from the conference committee passes both houses, it is ready for the final stage of the legislative process.

THE LAST STEPS

Even if a bill passes the House and Senate in identical form, one hurdle remains—the president, who has three options. If the bill meets his approval, the president will sign it, choosing the time and place most fitting—from a stroke of the pen late at night to a grand public ceremony with hundreds of spectators in the Rose Garden. Alternatively, the president can **veto** a bill, refusing to cooperate with Congress and sending it back to them. If both of the chambers pass the bill again by at least a two-thirds majority, the bill becomes law, overriding the president's veto. If the president does not act on a bill within ten days of receipt, the bill automatically becomes law unless Congress is in the last days of session. To keep Congress from sending a flood of bills to the president at the end of a term, the Constitution provides for the **pocket veto**. Thus, if Congress adjourns before the president has ten days to consider signing a measure, it automatically fails.

A BILL BECOMES TWO LAWS

If one were to research the fate of H.R. 2018, it would appear that the bill died in committee. In reality, however, the major components of the bill did become law. The provision to help states promote safe-havens programs became part of the Protecting Safe and Stable Families Act. Because this bill had broad bipartisan support, it came to a House vote under suspension of the rules on November 13, 2001. Easily garnering the two-thirds vote needed to pass, no one even requested a recorded vote. The bill then moved to the Senate. Democrat Harry Reid brought the bill before the Senate on December 13, 2001. After a series of floor speeches commending the bipartisan efforts behind the scenes on the bill, it passed by unanimous consent on December 13, 2001. Four days later, President Bush signed the bill, creating Public Law 107-133.[8]

The second provision from H.R. 2018, the request for the Department of Health and Human Services to conduct a study of the infant abandonment problem, was enfolded into the bill reauthorizing the Child Abuse Prevention and Treatment Act after the successful hearings highlighting the need for better data. First passed in the House by a vote of 411 to 5 on April 23, 2002, the so-called Keeping Children and Families Safe Act of 2002 never reached the Senate floor for a vote during the 107th Congress.

At the beginning of the 108th Congress, Representative Peter Hoekstra reintroduced the CAPTA reauthorization bill as H.R. 14. Identical to the version passed by the House the year before, the new bill contained the same section from Hart's original bill that requires the Secretary of Health and Human Services to conduct a study of infant abandonment and report the results to Congress. While this bill was working its way through the House, Senator Judd Gregg introduced a similar bill, S. 342, that was quickly reported out of committee. Gregg's bill passed by unanimous consent on March 19, 2003, and was sent to the House. Once in the other chamber, Hoekstra offered a substitute that replaced the Senate bill with the text of H.R. 14; it passed the House by voice vote. Because the House and Senate passed different versions of the bill, congressional leaders appointed a conference committee that forged a compromise. On June 17, 2003, the House agreed to the conference report by a vote of 421 to 3; the Senate agreed by unanimous consent two days later. With President Bush's signature, Public Law 108-36 went into effect.[9] Both components of Melissa Hart's original safe-havens bill were now law.

CHAPTER SUMMARY

Of the thousands of bills introduced each congressional session, only a few hundred become laws. Given this reality, members wanting to create new policies may need to find creative ways to navigate the legislative process. Representative Hart was determined to find a way for the federal government to assist safe-havens programs, so she and her staff worked behind the scenes to incorporate safe-havens provisions into a larger bill likely to succeed.

The traditional path for a bill to become a law begins with a member or senator officially introducing the measure in the chamber. Bills then proceed to committees, where the chair may agree to schedule hearings and markups. Committee staff offer members practical advice and suggest political strategy. If a majority of the committee votes favorably, the bill is reported to the chamber for consideration. Because each chamber follows its own procedure to move bills to the floor for debate and votes, the process in the rule-bound House is typically quicker and more regimented than that in the more traditional and deliberative Senate.

This chapter followed the Safe Havens Support Act beginning with its original introduction as H.R. 2018 through to the president's signature, illustrating one variant path for moving policy to final passage. By working behind the scenes to secure the support of committee leaders and their staff,

Hart shepherded the two core elements of H.R. 2018 into amendments to larger bills that became law.

NOTES

1. For an in-depth discussion of the committee system, see Christopher J. Deering and Steven S. Smith, *Committees in Congress*, 3rd ed. (Washington, D.C.: Congressional Quarterly Press, 1997).
2. Roger H. Davidson and Walter J. Oleszek, *Congress and Its Members*, 9th ed. (Washington, D.C.: Congressional Quarterly Press, 2004), 203.
3. Richard J. Fenno, *Congressmen in Committees* (Boston: Little, Brown, 1973), 1–2.
4. Theda Skocpol, *Boomerang: Health Care Reform and the Turn Against Government* (New York: W. W. Norton, 1997), 101–2.
5. John Boehner, Committee on Education and the Workforce, "House Subcommittee Hears Testimony on Legislation to Prevent Child Abuse and Neglect," press release, 2 August 2001 (accessed at http://edworkforce.house.gov/press/press107/capta8201.htm).
6. House Subcommittee on Select Education of the Committee on Education and the Workforce, 107th Congress, *Hearing on Prevention and Treatment of Child Abuse and Neglect: Policy Directions for the Future*, October 17, 2001, 10 (accessed at http://frwebgate.access.gpo.gov/cgi-bin/getdoc.cgi?dbname=107_house_hearings&docid=f:80041.pdf).
7. A definitive resource on congressional procedure is Walter Oleszek, *Congressional Procedures and the Policy Process*, 6th ed. (Washington, D.C.: Congressional Quarterly Press, 2004).
8. HR. 2873, 107th Congress (accessed a: http://thomas.loc.gov/cgi-bin/bdquerytr/z?d107:HR02873:@@@P).
9. S 342, 108th Congress (accessed at http://thomas.loc.gov/cgi-bin/bdquery/z?d108:SN00342:|TOM:/bss/d108query.html).

CONCLUSION

FROM INSPIRATION TO LEGISLATION

If one were to research H.R. 2018 in Thomas, the Library of Congress Web site that allows visitors to search the status of every bill ever introduced in the House or Senate, a quick glance would show that the Safe Havens Support Act failed to attract the attention of even a single House committee. As with so many aspects of the American political system, however, the real story of this bill was quite different than it might first appear. Just as Congresswoman Hart expected, H.R. 2018 made little progress through the House of Representatives as a stand-alone bill. The central policies included in it, however, became parts of two major legislative acts, one that passed in the 107th Congress and another that passed in the 108th Congress. A reporter listing Representative Hart's policy successes might miss the safe-havens issue completely, but the congresswoman and her staff know that her work in raising awareness of the problem of abandoned infants during her first term was a legislative success that led to important policy change.

This book has told the inside story of how an idea became a bill and how that bill became two laws. In this final chapter, we look back on the case study and ask, to what extent is this narrative typical of congressional action, and in what ways might this story be unique? In answering these questions, we consider some of the insights into real politics in America that we can learn from the tale of H.R. 2018. In particular, this chapter highlights some of the strengths of the political process, notes some of the limits of congressional politics, and offers a few caveats about generalizing from this one case study.

A Sum Greater than its Parts

Even the most charismatic legislator cannot succeed without the assistance of many other people; legislation is always a group effort. The safe-havens story demonstrates this principle in several ways. From the original letter that sparked the congresswoman's interest to the team of people who transformed Hart's ideas into words and actions, the ultimate success of H.R. 2018 was the result of many people's work.

The Importance of the Grassroots

In all likelihood, H.R. 2018 and the legislation it influenced would not have been possible without the initial concern raised by one person. As we saw in chapter 2, grassroots activist Patti Weaver cared enough about the abandoned-infants problem to establish a program designed to counteract the negative trends. She brought the issue to the attention of her elected officials, and many of them, including Hart, acted. Cynics may question the importance of any one person to the political process, but the story of this bill offers an important reminder that grassroots activism can indeed lead to policy change.

The Role of Expertise

Experts played a central role in both shaping abandoned-infants legislation and securing its passage. The original text of the relatively short and concise bill reflected the efforts of dozens of people. From the time that the congress-woman initially requested a draft of a bill, Hart's staff, committee staff, interest-group leaders, activists, and attorneys in the Office of Legislative Counsel all provided input that became part of H.R. 2018. Even lobbyists who are often derided for exerting unwelcome influence over the legislative process played an important role. As we saw in chapter 3, lobbyists can serve as important sources of data and information that assist legislators as they design policy. In the process of writing her bill, Hart relied on a team of experts who helped her refine and improve her ideas in order to craft a solid and workable bill.

Building and Maintaining Relationships

The story of this legislation is also the story of building and maintaining strong interpersonal relationships. Successful legislators often achieve their goals because they work well with others. Despite the intensity of partisan

politics described in chapter 6, Representatives Hart and Tubbs Jones part-
nered across the aisle and built a coalition of Republican and Democratic
support for their efforts. Maintaining friendships over time can also help
legislators achieve their goals. When Hart needed assistance from someone
on the Ways and Means Human Resources Subcommittee, for example, she
turned to her friend and former aide, Representative Phil English, to incorporate safe-havens provisions into another bill.

Building relationships is equally important for congressional staff members. Given the pressure of a member's schedule, successful legislators must
delegate detail work. Aides working on legislation rely on advice and assistance from experts within Congress and outside the institution; effective
congressional staff members continually build and maintain these working
relationships so that their bosses can achieve their goals. As detailed in
chapter 3, Hart's staff developed contacts with many policy experts, including
some potential opponents of the bill. These relationships led to improvements
in the text of the bill and created goodwill with policy experts who could have
opposed Hart's efforts.

SEEKING CREATIVE SOLUTIONS

This bill's route to final passage is also a reminder of the importance of
working with other legislators to find innovative ways to create new policy.
The odds of any single bill becoming law in a given congressional session
are very small; only 383 of the 9,130 bills introduced in the 107th Congress
were signed into law.[1] Hart was aware of this challenge, so she began her
work on what would become the Safe Havens Support Act seeking creative
options and alternative legislative paths that might help her achieve her
policy goal. Chapter 8 demonstrates the ways in which Hart combined
forces with committee staff and other members to find a way to include safe-
havens provisions in two major bills that were all but certain to become law.
As this case study shows, entrepreneurial legislators who are willing to
share credit with other members are much more likely to see their proposals
enacted.

THE LIMITS OF POLITICS

Although this book showcases many of the triumphs of politics, this story
also demonstrates some of the limits of politics and the political process.
Elected officials will not always achieve their goals, and government will not
provide a ready solution to every problem.

CONGRESSIONAL POWER AND WEAKNESS

Congress and its members work within the boundaries set by the Constitution. That is, even the most determined senator or member may discover that his or her idea is outside the scope of what Congress can or will do. This book considers the constraints of federalism, the division of power and sovereignty between state and national governments. As highlighted in chapter 5, states have jurisdiction over many spheres of law and policy that the national government rarely or never addresses. In the case of safe havens for abandoned infants, Hart learned the limits of federal power when she originally sought to change criminal law. She eventually created a bill that used federal government resources to assist states with safe-havens programs, but the boundaries of congressional powers limited her options.

COMPETITION FOR ATTENTION

Another limit on congressional action is competition. First, members and senators compete with each other for media attention. No news outlet, however comprehensive might be the coverage it seeks to provide, can track all the legislative efforts of 535 people. Individual legislators or groups of legislators working on the same issue try to raise awareness of their policy priorities, hoping that a particular issue will capture the attention of the media and the public. Only a few issues will capture national attention, however, so more legislators will lose this battle than will win.

Second, Congress as an institution competes for attention with other political actors and branches. The news media can report only a limited number of stories, so legislators vie for attention alongside the president, the Supreme Court, and executive branch agencies. As discussed in chapter 7, the president receives far more news coverage than Congress. A single individual backed by a powerful staff with significant resources, the president is a natural focal point for news coverage. Members of Congress, in contrast, represent diverse views. Reporters looking to write simple stories find the complexities of Congress difficult to navigate. Furthermore, legislators with opposing policy positions compete with one another for media coverage at the same time that they wage turf battles over public policy.

IDEALS AND COMPROMISE

The safe-havens story also highlights the role of compromise in politics. Elected officials quickly learn the maxim that effective legislators will compromise in order to secure results. Hart learned this lesson early in her congressional career. Although she never wavered from the ideal of saving abandoned babies, she was open to changing a few details of her proposal to gain the political leverage necessary to succeed. More often than not, flexibility in achieving policy goals is the best way to achieve legislative success. Legislators, therefore, must carefully weigh the alternatives, determining what compromises are acceptable to further their policy goals versus what changes would violate fundamental principles.

A Few Caveats

This insider view of the process offers important insights into the dynamics of everyday politics on Capitol Hill, but it tells the story of only one legislator and the journey of one of her policy ideas. Given the diversity of bills introduced in Congress and the outside pressures and factors that affect their success, one should be careful about hastily generalizing from this one case study.

The story of H.R. 2018 unfolds almost entirely in the House of Representatives. The general process of translating an idea into a bill follows a similar path in either chamber, but the particularities of the House and Senate, compared in part in chapter 8, are quite different. The House, for example, is more regimented and rule bound; the Senate is more informal, and individual senators wield more power than their counterparts in the House. The specifics of how Hart navigated the politics of her bill necessarily reflect the culture and context of the House of Representatives.

In addition, the Safe Havens Support Act created little controversy. Democrats and Republicans easily found common ground on this bill because of its limited scope and broad appeal. Most of the bills enacted into law each congressional session are "small" bills like H.R. 2018, bipartisan efforts to make incremental or symbolic policy changes. Many other legislative proposals, however, are far more complex and contentious than Hart's bill, so they would necessarily follow a different path than that of safe havens. Media accounts often spotlight congressional action on these broader, grander legislative proposals, but, more often than not, such controversial legislation fails.

Conclusion

The typical introductory American government textbook includes a diagram that illustrates how a bill becomes a law, but very few resources demonstrate how an idea can become a bill. This book has done just that, tracing the story of how one woman arrived on Capitol Hill and learned to navigate the legislative process. The story of the success of the Safe Havens Support Act is a testament to the power of ideas, the importance of individual citizens who want to make a difference, the passion of legislators to achieve their goals, and the triumph of the legislative process.

NOTE

1. Jennifer E. Manning, "Congressional Statistics: Bills Introduced and Laws Enacted, 1947–2003," *CRS Report for Congress 96-727 C*, March 3, 2004, 3.

APPENDIX A

TEXT OF THE ORIGINAL
SAFE HAVENS SUPPORT ACT

107th CONGRESS

1st Session

H.R. 2018

To authorize States to use funds provided under the program of block grants to States for temporary assistance for needy families to support infant safe haven programs.

IN THE HOUSE OF REPRESENTATIVES

MAY 25, 2001

Ms. HART (for herself, Mrs. JONES of Ohio, Mr. WELDON of Pennsylvania, Mr. BACHUS, Mr. ENGLISH, Mr. ADERHOLT, Mr. SMITH of New Jersey, Mr. PITTS, Mr. STEARNS, Mrs. JO ANN DAVIS of Virginia, Mr. HOEKSTRA, Mrs. MYRICK, Ms. ROS-LEHTINEN, Mr. SOUDER, Ms. PRYCE of Ohio, Mr. WELDON of Florida, Ms. JACKSON-LEE of Texas, Ms. LEE, Mr. GREENWOOD, and Mr. RYUN of Kansas) introduced the following bill; which was referred to the Committee on Ways and Means, and in addition to the Committee on Education and the Workforce, for a period to be subsequently determined by the Speaker, in each case for consideration of such provisions as fall within the jurisdiction of the committee concerned.

A BILL

To authorize States to use funds provided under the program of block grants to States for temporary assistance for needy families to support infant safe haven programs.

Be it enacted by the Senate and House of Representatives of the United States of America in Congress assembled,

SECTION 1. SHORT TITLE.

This Act may be cited as the "Safe Havens Support Act of 2001."

SEC. 2. TANF FUNDS AUTHORIZED TO BE USED FOR INFANT SAFE HAVEN PROGRAMS.

Section 404(a) of the Social Security Act (42 U.S.C. 604(a)) is amended—
  (1) by striking "or" at the end of paragraph (1);
  (2) by striking the period at the end of paragraph (2) and inserting "; or"; and
  (3) by adding at the end the following:
  "(3) to support an infant safe haven program."
(b) INFANT SAFE HAVEN PROGRAM DEFINED—Section 419 of such Act (42 U.S.C. 619) is amended by adding at the end the following:
    "(6) INFANT SAFE HAVEN PROGRAM—
        "(A) IN GENERAL—The term "infant safe haven program" means any program or activity which—
            "(i) provides a way for a parent to safely relinquish a newborn infant at a safe haven designated pursuant to a State law, or an agreement approved by a local prosecutor, which—
                "(I) prescribes, or under which are prescribed, procedures for lawfully relinquishing such an infant; and
                "(II) provides that a parent who lawfully relinquishes such an infant shall be immune from prosecution for child abandonment based on such conduct, or shall be entitled to raise such conduct as an affirmative defense in such a prosecution;
            "(ii) provides a designated toll-free information line for the purpose of directing individuals to locations that are authorized to accept newborn infants relinquished pursuant to such a law or agreement and to provide information about infant relinquishment laws or agreements;
            "(iii) provides for the education and training of individuals who are authorized to accept newborn infants relinquished pursuant to such a law or agreement, to familiarize the individuals with the procedures prescribed by or under the law or agreement for accepting, and caring for a parent who is relinquishing, such an infant; or
            "(iv) recruits and trains health and social services personnel to work with relinquished or abandoned infants, their families, and prospective adoptive families.
        "(B) SUPPORT—The term "support" means, with respect to an infant safe haven program, to develop, carry out, or inform any segment of the public about such a program.

"(C) RELATED TERMS—In subparagraph (A):
  "(i) NEWBORN INFANT—The term "newborn infant" means a child who is not more than 30 days old.
  "(ii) RELINQUISH—The term "relinquish" means to surrender physical custody."

SEC. 3. STUDY OF INFANTS WHO ARE ABANDONED, RELINQUISHED, OR DECEASED.

(a) STUDY—The Secretary of Health and Human Services shall conduct a study to determine—
  (1) an estimate of the annual number of infants who are relinquished, abandoned, or found dead in the United States within 1 year after their birth;
  (2) an estimate of the annual number of such infants who are victims of homicide; and
  (3) characteristics and demographics of parents who have abandoned an infant in the United States within 1 year after its birth.

(b) REPORT TO THE CONGRESS—Not later than 18 months after the date of the enactment of this Act, and annually during the next 2 years, the Secretary of Health and Human Services shall submit to the Congress a written report that describes the findings of the study required by subsection (a), and contains such recommendations as the Secretary deems appropriate.

GLOSSARY

501(c)(3) status: granted to non-profit organizations organized under 501(c)(3) section of the Internal Revenue code; allows organizations to offer donors tax deductions for charitable giving

501(c)4 status: granted to non-profit organization organized under 501(c)4 section of the Internal Revenue code; can lobby, but contributions are not tax deductible

appropriations bills: annual bills passed by Congress that allocate specific amounts of money to programs authorized by previous legislation

authorization of appropriations: legislative approval that gives the federal government the authority to spend stated sums of money for a given purpose; the first step in the appropriations process

beats: assignments by news organizations to focus journalists' work; the location or subject matter that a journalist follows and reports

block grants: federal grants that give money to states in large "blocks" with a broad set of guidelines; provide states flexibility in spending federal funds

broadcast markets: the geographic area across which television and radio stations broadcast their signals

calendar of motions to discharge committees: the legislative schedule in the House that determines the voting schedule for formal proposals supported by a majority of the chamber's members to force movement of bills "stuck" in committee

categorical grants: federal grants that distribute money to recipients with specific instructions for how the money must be used; often require matching funds

caucuses: unofficial partnerships that may evolve into more structured groups with regular meeting times and definable membership boundaries; play an important role in shaping politics on Capitol Hill

centralized structure: the most popular form of organization for House and Senate offices; senior staff members and the district director report to the chief of staff who reports to the senator or representative

chairman's mark amendment: the initial changes to a bill suggested by a committee chair at the beginning of a markup session

.kbook members: members of organizations who participate primarily by paying membership fees, leaving lobbying and advocacy to political professionals

chief of staff: the congressional staff member who directs the operations of a congressional office; the final authority on all issues in absence of the member; sometimes called the administrative assistant

citizen groups: membership organizations formed around a shared sense of community or common interest

coalitions: partnerships between interest groups who work together to achieve common goals; sometimes form across ideological and party lines

committee chair: the congressional member of the majority party selected to oversee a committee's work; exerts great control over the legislative process by choosing what bills to consider, presiding over committee business, and scheduling meetings

Committee of the Whole: the forum through which members of the House debate and amend legislation under a different set of rules that expedite their work; must consider all bills that include taxes or spending

committee reports: formal written reports, including transcripts, recorded votes, and explanations, that often accompany complex bills

committees: working groups of legislators that process legislative proposals; divided by subject matter to help distribute the workload and help members and Senators develop policy expertise

communications director: the congressional staff member who coordinates media operations and works actively to maximize both the quantity and the quality of a legislator's media coverage

companion bills: identical or similar legislative proposals that work their way through the House and Senate simultaneously

competitive grant: a federal grant that requires recipients to compete for funding through the submission of applications that explain how the money would be used and why the recipient is well-suited to provide the expected service

conference committee: a special form of joint committee that convenes temporarily to reach compromise language on bills originally passed in different forms by the House and Senate

conference report: the compromise reached in a conference committee that includes new wording of a bill for each chamber to consider in a simple up-or-down vote

congressional membership organizations (CMOs): structured groups of legislators that replaced legislative service organizations (LSOs); provide a forum for like-minded legislators to work together on policy initiatives

Congressional Research Service (CRS): a nonpartisan organization that provides comprehensive and reliable analysis, research and information services to members of Congress and their staff

constituency careers: the professional activities members of Congress pursue in their home districts or states to help secure reelection

constituent newsletters: mailings that update constituents on recent legislation, government programs that may be of interest, upcoming meetings in the district, and any other issues the legislator chooses to highlight; typically sent about twice a year

corrections calendar: the legislative schedule in the House that receives noncontroversial bills intended to make minor corrections to federal rules, regulations, and court decisions; the bills on this calendar may be considered for a vote on the second and fourth Tuesdays of each month

cosponsors: congressional members who add their names in support of legislation; an indicator of strong support for a bill

counsel: lawyers hired by committees for legal advice; often assist the chair and the ranking member during committee proceedings to provide advice on parliamentary procedure

critical realignment theory: the theory that one of the two major political parties dominates American national politics for about a generation before losing power in a transformative election

dealignment: a trend that occurs when neither major political party controls both houses of Congress and the presidency over a period of time

"dear colleague" letters: generic letters sent to all members of the chamber briefly describing a bill and what is proposes to accomplish; a popular method for soliciting cosponsors for a piece of legislation

definitions section: a section in either the beginning or end of most bills that clarifies and defines potentially ambiguous terms used within the bill

devolution: the redistribution of federal powers and/or funds to the states

direct lobbying: the legal term referring to paid professionals contacting policymakers or their staff members with the goal of influencing policy

divided government: split power between Republicans and Democrats, with power shifting between the two major parties, and neither party dominating the executive and legislative branches of government

.tive calendar: the legislative schedule in the Senate for pending .ominations, resolutions, and treaties; holds the measures that offer advice or consent on presidential actions after they have been reported out of committee until they are considered for a vote by the chamber

editorials: articles that openly express the opinions of their authors to present the arguments from one perspective on an issue or topic

federalism: a system of government in which sovereign powers are shared between a national government and state governments

findings: a section included in the beginning of many bills that includes factual statements, data, and/or reasoning explaining the goals and purpose of the bill

formula grant: grants that disperse money using some kind of arithmetic calculation

functional structure: the least common form of organization for House and Senate offices; the heads of both the Washington and district offices report to the chief of staff and the member

grassroots lobbying: the process of persuading individual voters to pressure their elected officials with the goal of influencing policy

grassroots movements: individuals working at a local level who seek to enact social and political change

guest editorials: opinion essays that present the perspective of a person not affiliated with a newspaper; a popular format for legislators who want to bring attention to their favorite initiatives

hopper: the box located next to the rostrum at the front of the House chamber in which members or delegates place a signed copy of their bills, thus introducing legislation into the chamber

house calendar: the legislative schedule in the House that receives bills that do not require consideration by the Committee of the Whole

infant safe havens: state laws or local programs that provide immunity or affirmative defense from prosecution to a parent who safely relinquishes an unwanted infant at a designated location

interest group: a group unified by a common bond that takes action to influence public policy in its favor

joint committee: committees that include members from both the House and the Senate

laboratories of democracy: a metaphor used to describe the way that states serve as a resource for testing the effectiveness of different ways to achieve similar policy goals

legislative assistants: congressional staff members who manage and research specific issues for a member of Congress, meet with constituents and lobbyists, and build support for legislation

legislative correspondent: the congressional staff member who manages office correspondence, responding to constituent mail that legislators receive

legislative counsel: offices in both the House and the Senate that provide teams of trained attorneys to help legislators transform their policy ideas into standard legislative language

legislative director: the congressional staff member who directs the legislative agenda and helps promote the member's policy priorities, monitors the legislative calendar, and oversees other members of the legislative staff

legislative history: the background of past attempts to address a policy issue; the record of events surrounding successful and unsuccessful legislation

legislative service organizations (LSOs): structured caucuses of legislators with offices and staff on Capitol Hill; abolished by reforms in the 104th Congress (1995–1996)

letters to the editor: essays that share space with the opinion columns in the editorial/opinion section of a newspaper; provide readers an opportunity to express their views

lobbying: the process of attempting to influence change in legislation or public policy

majority leader: elected by the party with the most members in each chamber; responsible for scheduling activity on the floor of his or her chamber

majority staff: the groups of professionals who work on behalf of a committee chair and the members from the majority party; typically has more resources and office space than the minority staff

matching funds: funds to help pay for a project or service that are required by some legislation; grant recipients must "match" federal dollars with their own contributions

marginal seat: an electoral district in which the incumbent received less than 55 or 60 percent of the vote in the last election, indicating the likely competitiveness of the next election

markup: the stage of the committee process where committee members review the proposed text of a bill and decide on the final language to be sent to the chamber for debate

media advisory: a type of press release that alerts the news media to an upcoming event and includes essential information such as the date, time, and location

media entrepreneurs: politicians who actively cultivate media opportunities to promote policy goals, seeking the attention of media outlets that are most likely to influence elite opinion

member as manager: an uncommon form of organization for House offices; every staff person reports to the member of Congress

minority leader: the legislative leader elected by the party with the least members in each chamber; presents the case of the opposition party, identifies weaknesses in policies supported by majority party and offers alternative policy plans

minority staff: a separate office of professionals who work on behalf of the ranking member and committee members from the minority party

motion to suspend the rules: a common mechanism that allows the House to consider uncontroversial bills with relative speed; requires a two-thirds majority to pass such bills

news hooks: stories from recent and breaking news that could be connected, or hooked to a policy or activity that congressional members or communications staff want to promote

office manager: the congressional staff member who assists with the daily functions of running an office including payroll, accounts, and paper-work

original cosponsors: the members and senators who add their names in support of a bill before its official introduction in the chamber

partisanship: strong, often fervent support for and devotion to a particular political party; often leads to divisiveness and difficulty working across party lines

party caucuses: groups of all of the members and senators of each party who formally gather to plan political strategy and share information; also known as party conferences

party unity votes: congressional floor votes in which a majority of Republican legislators vote on the opposite side of a majority of their Democratic counterparts

pocket veto: the constitutional provision requiring the automatic failure of an unsigned bill if Congress adjourns before the president has ten days to consider signing the measure

political action committees (PAC): organizations who raise money to contribute to political parties and candidates for federal, state, and local offices

president pro-tempore: the longest-serving member of the majority party; assumes authority as presiding officer of the Senate in the absence of the vice president

press conference: a targeted event where journalists are provided with an easy news story and allowed to ask questions

press kits: packets of information distributed to journalists attending a special event; the provided materials are intended for reporters to reference as they write stories about the event

press release: a prefabricated news story distributed to the media for their use; a primary tool of the press secretary's trade

press secretary: sometimes known as the director of communications; the congressional staff member who handles all interaction with the news media; may also serve as a speechwriter

primary cosponsor: a legislator, usually from the opposite political party of a bill's initial sponsor, who joins in support of a bill and agrees to champion it among fellow partisans

private calendar: the legislative schedule in the House for all private bills; bills on this calendar may be brought to the floor for consideration on the first or third Tuesday of each month.

professional staff: congressional committee and subcommittee professionals with expertise on specific policies and legislation within that committee's jurisdiction

pseudo-event: staged events created for the purpose of generating media coverage to enable politicians to draw attention to their work

public hearing: an open committee session for discussion of a proposal and its possible implications

ranking member: the congressional member of the minority party with the longest continuous service on the panel who acts as the spokesperson and provides leadership for fellow partisans

reauthorization: the process of extending funding for a program established by a public law set to expire on a given date

rules: resolutions that allow the House to consider bills without following the order on House calendars; help structure and manage floor debate

Rules Committee: the House committee that writes resolutions for special consideration that may include provisions for the length of debate on a bill, the number of amendments allowed, and the order of consideration of amendments; most bills reach the House floor through this committee

safe seat: an electoral district in which the incumbent received more than 60 percent of the vote in the last election; assumed to be a guaranteed win for the incumbent in the next election

scheduler: the congressional staff member who manages the member's time by sorting through invitations the member receives, turning down most requests and accommodating some

select committee: temporary congressional committees that primarily hold hearings and highlight issues; often form for a stated purpose and disband after they have completed their appointed task

senate legislative calendar: the Senate legislative schedule that receives all bills that are eligible for floor consideration in the Senate

site visit: a tour a legislator makes of a local business, community center, or school; members of the news media often accompany legislators and report on the event

Speaker of the House: the elected leader in the House who also serves as the head of the majority party; the most powerful and visible member of Congress who officially presides over business in the chamber

special resolutions: also known as rules; allow the House to consider bills without following the order on House calendars; help structure and manage floor debate

sponsor: the congressional member who writes a bill and presents it before the chamber for consideration; serves as the primary spokesperson and advocate for the bill

staff assistant: the congressional staff member who sits in the front office, answers the phones, and greets visitors to a Congressional office; typical route of entry to work on Capitol Hill

staff director: the person who runs a committee office and reports to the chair or ranking member; has duties and responsibilities similar to the chief of staff in a legislator's office

standing committee: permanent committees with fixed subject-matter jurisdictions that receive proposals for legislation and process them into bills

straight news: the reporting of news events without discernible bias or spin; objective accounts answering who, what, when, and where

subcommittees: subdivisions of committees that serve to further divide labor, have more specific subject-matter jurisdictions, and report to the parent committee

syndicated columns: opinion essays by a specific writer; sold to newspapers to reproduce on a daily or weekly basis

systems administrator: the congressional staff member who manages technology and computing services in the office

technical amendments: legislation intended to make small changes designed to fix unanticipated problems in existing law; typically uncontroversial

technical assistance: the provision of education, training, and other forms of assistance that help state governments or organizations provide services more effectively

unanimous consent: a Senate norm that requires the agreement of everyone present for business to proceed

unanimous consent agreements (UCAs): Senate provisions that work similar to rules in the House by limiting debate and setting parameters on amendments

union calendar: the legislative schedule in the House that includes most public bills; the bills are numbered in the order received and await further legislative action

unlimited debate: a Senate tradition that recognizes the right of each senator to speak on the floor without limitation

veto: the presidential power to overturn a bill passed by Congress; legislators can override the veto if both chambers pass the bill again by at least a two-thirds majority

washington careers: the professional activities members of Congress pursue in Washington in order to achieve their policy goals and build power and influence within their chamber

washington/district-state parity structure: a form of organization for House and Senate offices in which Washington staff members report to the chief or staff and district or state office staff report to the district director, giving the Washington and district offices equal authority

whips: legislative leaders elected by each party whose primary responsibilities include mobilizing votes and disseminating information to fellow partisans

wire service: a subscription news service that provides media outlets access to news stories they can reprint in their own papers

INDEX